W9-AMB-025

Principled Leadership Practical Counsel for Godly Leaders

by
Bernard A. Warren

Based on St. Paul's gritty letter to Titus, his friend and colleague in ministry on the Island of Crete, this little book offers help to those who are called to the tough job of leading others with grace, insight, and steadfast integrity. It also will help to guide those preparing for leadership and those who are called to be followers.

LEADERSHIP

PRINCIPLED
Leadership
practical counsel for Godly leaders

Bernard Warren

PRINCIPLED LEADERSHIP
Copyright © 2008, Bezek Foundation

All Scripture quotations, unless otherwise specified, are from the *Revised Standard Version* of the Bible (Copyright © 1946, 1952; © 1971, 1973 by the Division of Christian Education of the National Council of the Churches of Christ in the United States of America.) • Scriptures marked NIV are from *The Holy Bible, New International Version.* Copyright © 1973, 1978, 1984 International Bible Society. Used by permission of Zondervan Publishing House. All rights reserved. • Scripture taken from *The Message*, copyright © by Eugene H. Peterson, 1993, 1994, 1995. Used by permission of NavPress Publishing Group. • Scripture quotations marked NKJV are taken from the New King James Version. Copyright © 1979, 1980, 1982. Thomas Nelson Inc., Publishers. • Scripture quotations marked KJV *The Holy Bible, King James Version.* Copyright © 1977, 1984, Thomas Nelson Inc., Publishers. • Scripture quotations marked TLB are taken from *The Living Bible.* Copyright © 1971 by Tyndale House Publishers, Wheaton, Illinois 60187. All rights reserved. (Some scriptural references are paraphrased by the author.)

National Library of Canada Cataloguing in Publication
Warren, Bernard A. (Bernard Arthur) 1927-
Principled Leadership: Practical Counsel for Godly Leaders/ Bernard A. Warren.Includes biographical references
First Printing January 2008
Second Printing March 2008

ISBN: 978-1-55452-236-1
Published by Bezek Foundation Incorporated
Printed in Ontario, Canada by Essence Publishing

Dedication

Wisdom says, *"Iron sharpens iron"* (Proverbs 27:17). Fred and Collette Christmas usually join Dorla and me to watch the Super Bowl. For more than thirty years, and over many cups of coffee, Fred and I have discussed faith, history, politics, and sports. Through his life and work in Leadership Ministries, he influences many men towards a more faithful walk with the Lord Jesus Christ. This book is dedicated to my friend Fred Christmas.

Contents

Acknowledgements

Betty Saito, with her eagle eye has, over the years, faithfully read and re-read my books to correct the spelling, punctuation, and sentence structure. Laurna Tallman, with her long experience in professional editing, has been helpful in adjusting the order and flow of the manuscript.

I am also grateful to my friends Justin Cooper, a leader in the academic world, and Robert Hayman, a leader in the world of construction, for their commendations on the back cover.

Preface

This little book was birthed by an even smaller book, a letter from St. Paul to his friend and colleague, Titus. Found in the New Testament, Paul's letter speaks to the condition of the churches on the small Greek island of Crete. Titus is their overseer. All was not well in those churches, and Paul instructs Titus to "mend what is defective" in them. Building on St. Paul's experience and insights and drawing on my own ministry of leadership, I identify some defects in our churches and offer godly remedies to faulty ways in which some leaders function today, not only in the church but in every organization or business where people work together.

The problems Paul identifies are timeless. In every generation, we find evidence of leaders who led well. Others exhibit defects of character, have strange ideas, lack certainty of purpose, and have little vision. Today, we need people who, like Titus, are willing to do some mending of that which is not yet right. In the meantime God continues to work with imperfect people to fulfill His intentions in His time.

Whether you are a man or a woman called into leadership, following Paul's counsel in his letter to Titus will enable you to do so with increasing integrity, insight, and grace. It seems that those who understand the requirements of leadership also are able to accept graciously the leading of others and to support their leaders with patience and enthusiasm.

1

Introducing Titus

Early and Modern Church Leadership

The New Testament describes many different ways in which the early Christians formed the church. In the old days, there were many leadership styles and a great diversity in organizational structures. The early church had apostles, elders, deacons, bishops, pastors, and a variety of overseers of other ranks. Someone who cared to do so searched the New Testament and detected twenty-two different types of organization and government among those early churches.

Today, we can match those and have added a few of our own. We now have popes, moderators, and metropolitans; cardinals, archbishops, presidents, priests, and monsignors. There are wardens, deans, stewards, managers, superintendents, and worship leaders.

Let's first take a look and see where Titus fits in to the early church structure; then we will look at the twenty-first-century church and the problems and opportunities we face.

The Churches on Crete

Titus was directly under the authority of St. Paul, the apostle who appointed him overseer of the churches they had evangelized on the island of Crete. We know very little about these churches.

From the tone of Paul's letter, we can assume that many of them weren't doing well. In this letter to Titus, Paul speaks of character and conduct defects in some of their leaders. He also mentions problems in their organization and is concerned about their doctrine. Paul instructs Titus to fix things. *"The reason I left you in Crete was that you might straighten out what was left unfinished and appoint elders in every town, as I directed you"* (Titus 1:5 NIV). By studying Paul's letter, we get some clues about how we might fix things in our churches and other organizations too.

Titus

Imagine listening to Titus as he introduces himself to us, tells how he got started in his job, and shares something of his plans for dealing with the defects in the churches on Crete.

"My name is Titus, and I'm a middle-aged Greek widower. Right now I'm the overseer of the churches on this little island of Crete. It's not a very prestigious job. The churches are small and not very mature. Sometimes I don't think they take me very seriously.

"How did I get this job? You've heard about the Jewish teacher Paul, haven't you? He's a tent maker by trade, and I met him at my textile arcade in the market in Rome when he was looking for felted wool. I carry a variety of local and imported materials, and while I was selling him fabric he led me to Jesus, the Jewish teacher whose followers he had been trying to exterminate. He taught me new ways to pray.

"To make a long story short, we got to know one another and I left my business to be run by my children, Felix and Miranda, who are grown now, in order to go with Paul to Asia Minor. We carried the Good News about Jesus and helped the new believers to organize their churches. That was my first trip with this fiery ambassador of the true God.

"I started to work with Paul about the year 60 A.D. by your calendar. I was a willing horse, so he gave me some tough jobs to do. Because my family is grown, I am free to come and go. Once he sent me to that rowdy city of Corinth with a letter to the church there. That was some letter! It blistered them for their immorality and the stupid ways they had acted in the midst of celebrating the Lord's Supper—some of them getting stone-drunk on the wine (1 Corinthians 11:21). He asked me to wait until his letter was read to the church and then bring back their response. They gathered in a room and closed the door. I stood outside listening. I could hear them shouting. Then things quieted down, and finally they gave me their answer in a letter that I took back to Paul. It proved to be a helpful exchange of views (2 Corinthians 7:8). I have kept copies of Paul's letters together with some other important writings.

"Concerning my friend and mentor Paul, I want you to know that he wasn't just a now-and-then tent maker sending out some of his friends on missionary trips; he did a lot of the heavy lifting himself. It was about a year ago when he said, 'You've got some good connections in Crete, let's go there and share the Gospel with them, and see if we can establish a few churches.' So off we went. We did meet with some small success. But Paul moves according to his discernment of the Spirit of Jesus and soon headed off on another trip. He left me behind to work with the few churches we had established.

"It wasn't easy working with the Cretans. For one thing, the new groups of converts were scattered across the island. They believed all kinds of things. They worshipped strange gods and carried out some weird practices. One of their own prophets, Epimenides, 500 years before had cursed them by declaring, 'Cretans are always liars, evil beasts, lazy gluttons' (Titus 1:12). That had stuck. Those who joined the churches brought their troubles with them. After a few months, I was discouraged, but Paul hadn't forgotten me. He sent me a letter. It was not exactly a 'feel-good' letter, but it was helpful: I needed to appoint local leaders, and he outlined some standards for those who could become leaders in the church.

"If I did what he asked in his letter, I would probably have to ease out some men who are in self-appointed leadership. And I might have to get some really capable people to start doing what they are being called by God to do. My job won't be easy. But you don't say 'No' to Paul. So rather than travel around to all the churches trying to teach the locals the things that Paul wrote about, I decided to invite the key men and women from those scattered congregations to come together for a teaching retreat where we could talk about some important issues.

"What about Crete? Well, it's not exactly the centre of the world. It's just a small Greek island in the Mediterranean Sea about 200 miles due south of Athens. It's about 150 miles long and 20 miles wide. It's not very populated, and most of the people are farmers. Because the population is pretty stretched out, I decided that if I wanted to reach all the church leaders, it would be easier to bring them together than for me to visit all their churches. It was worth a try. So I sent letters to the 11 churches on the island. Here's what I wrote:-

To the leaders of the churches on the island of Crete:
I have been trying to help the churches on our island grow and become mature. Over the past few months, we haven't seen much progress. However, I have just received a letter from our brother Paul with specific instructions for me as your overseer and for you as church leaders that will be of help to us. In his letter, he said the reason he left me on the island was to 'fix what is defective in our churches and make sure that there is proper leadership in each congregation.' I know this could upset some of you, but Paul has some clear ideas about how

things should be. In his letter are helpful insights concerning the roles and character qualifications of leaders.

So I am inviting one or two leaders from each church on the island to join together here at Fair Havens where we will discuss the contents of Paul's letter. Be prepared to be shaken up a bit because, as you know, Paul doesn't soften the truth. Giving you time to travel, we'll assemble on the second day after the celebration of the resurrection. Christians here will provide food and lodging for you for the four days we plan to be together. There should be about twenty of us if there are two representatives from every church. I look forward to seeing you.

Your brother in the Lord, Titus.

"Well, there were eighteen who came, and we went to work. As we got into it, a few got angry and left early when their leadership qualifications were questioned. They likely went home and said that we were meddling in their affairs. But those who stayed agreed that it was helpful to be together and study Paul's instructions. We prayed together three times each day. I gave talks based on the letter and asked them to share these things with their people back home, promising to visit each of them in turn according to the schedule we drew up. I have real hope that these people will change their own lives and bring Jesus to many others here on Crete."

Here We Are in the Twenty-first Century...

The things Paul wrote that Titus and his fellow Christians must have discussed were relevant not only to their day but apply to us as well. Under the skin, we are all alike and relationship issues are the same the world over and throughout the ages. God's principles do not change. So we can look at our organizations and see what Paul says that might help both Titus and us improve the ways we do things.

2

Leaders of Integrity

Straight Talk About Integrity

St. Paul did not mince words in his letter to Titus assigning him his task. He wrote, "The reason I left you behind in Crete was that you would set right what was defective and finish what was left undone." He continued, "and that you might appoint elders and set them over churches in every city as I directed you, men of unquestionable integrity" (Titus 1:5-6 author's paraphrase). Some of the problems in the churches were caused by flawed leadership. One with authority who recognizes defects in the church must lovingly and prayerfully deal with those who are responsible for them—the troublemaker, the immoral, the uncommitted, the incompetent, or the spiritual saboteur. Titus was mandated to assess the character, attitude, and ability of each leader. Then, he was to confirm that leader and correct or replace him. Today, in the church, we have presbyteries, bishops, superintendents, or other officials as overseers of churches. Sometimes they know what's actually going on, sometimes not. Sometimes they act, sometimes they do not.

Integrity is vital in the character of the leader, not only for performing in that position, but also because that enables the leader to require integrity in others. Not much good will happen in the fellowship if the leader will not seek out sources of distress in herself or himself and deal with them. Not much good will happen in the group if the leader is not a person of integrity. Wisdom says, *"Good leaders abhor wrongdoing at all times; sound leadership has a moral foundation"* (Proverbs 16:12 The Message).

Readiness to Lead

Back in the tenth century, England had a king named Ethelred the Unready. Perhaps I was like Ethelred when I was living in Sudbury and joined the Barber-Shoppers, a men's singing group. One evening, our leader didn't show up and I was pushed into the job. It was a near disaster. There was little sweet harmony that night! I was ill equipped to lead—but no one else was willing. Thus, some people get pushed into leadership before they are ready. When no one with much experience is available, the group can only pray that the untested leader will grow into the job without doing too much damage. A person may be gifted for leadership but not be yet well trained or ready for leadership.

On the other hand, a person may want to lead but not be suitable or ready. Paul warned his friend Timothy about elevating a man too quickly. "He must not be a new convert lest he become puffed up and conceited for being chosen so soon" (1 Timothy 3:6 author's paraphrase). He would display more ego than wisdom. One who attains a high position of Christian leadership must be aware that a fall (and too many do fall) is a long way down and many naive followers will fall along with their undependable head. Such tumbles bring public reproach upon the Gospel.

Testing and Growth

There needs to be a time of testing before a person is given heavy responsibilities. Jesus, in telling a parable about servants and their talents, said of the one who invested them best, *"Well done, good and faithful servant; you have been faithful over a little, I will set you over much"* (Matthew 25:21). The faithful servant took risks. Taking risks is part of growing and maturing. It is a test of courage that every leader needs. But giving a person too much responsibility before she or he has proven faithful and competent in a lesser role puts too much at risk and can create major problems. The person who will serve faithfully in a low-level position is eligible to be moved up to the next level of authority. But avoid the "Peter principle," which holds that people tend to be promoted until they reach a level beyond their competence. Know when not to accept more responsibility than you can handle. *"The wise shall inherit glory: but shame shall be the promotion of fools"* (Proverbs 3:35 KJV).

Critical Situations

A crisis of leadership can arise when the Holy Spirit brings more lambs into the fold than can be nurtured in any traditional way by mature shepherds. Rapid growth of the church requires something like a grade two student being the only one available to teach a grade one student. *Christian Week* recently received a report from the Bangladesh Baptist Fellowship that "shows an increase from 12 churches to 456 since 1980. This kind of growth inevitably creates issues as leaders take time to emerge and to mature." May God give us more problems like theirs!

In the closing paragraphs of his letter, Paul gives Titus a surprise. He says, *"When I send Artemas or Tychicus to you, do your best to come to me at Nicopolis..."* (Titus 3:12). Whoa! Titus is being replaced. That happens. Sometimes it is a promotion, sometimes the opposite. Often it comes without warning. Perhaps Titus had done what he could in Crete and a new leader might help the churches take the next step in maturity or outreach. We, as leaders, are not indispensable. Our roots must remain in God, not in our position.

Dreams Without Substance

A young man came to our Bezek Retreat Centre one afternoon all excited. He said, "The Lord told me I was to set up a network of Christian radio stations across Canada. I need your help."

I said, "Sounds impressive. Right now we are sending out a mailing. Take a chair and put stamps on these envelopes while we talk."

He was greatly insulted. "I'm going to build a network of Christian radio stations. I don't put on stamps." Finally, I convinced him to help us while we talked. He sulked as he put stamps on envelopes—some crooked, some sideways, some upside down. No minor tasks for him, for he was going to be the CEO of his dream radio network (with major help from us, of course). He left in a huff when we wouldn't promise total support. I didn't hold out much hope for his dream. He wanted to be a general before he proved himself a good foot soldier. In business, his approach only works if you're the boss's son.

At Bezek, even though I was the director, it was my responsibility to get the garbage out. Doing some grubby hands-on service helped to keep my ego in check.

Whom Do You Spend Time With?

The Psalmist, concerned about character, wrote, "Blessed is the man who does not walk with ungodly men seeking their counsel, nor stands idling with sinners discussing schemes to get rich, or sits around agreeing with scoffers who sneer at God. But he takes delight in God's ways of doing things and he continuously ponders and practices them. He is like a tree planted by a clear stream of water, which produces good fruit and does not dry up in times of severe drought" (Psalm 1:1-3 author's paraphrase).

Of course, we spend time with unbelievers, not to agree with them but to make our case for the Gospel and suffer abuse for it if we must. The person of integrity is one who can stand among those who belittle Christian beliefs and, with grace and clarity, declare the Word of the Lord and give good reasons why he or she believes it. A dictionary definition of *integrity* is "uprightness of character, honesty, steadfastness in the truth," and suggested synonyms are *fidelity, justice, virtue,* and *reliability.* The word comes from the same root as *integrate,* which simply means "getting all the parts together." Every Christian needs someone to whom an account of attitudes and actions can be given, lest she or he fall into self-deception. We need someone who will help us apply difficult scriptures. I came across this one: *"A faithful follower of the Lord is one who keeps a promise even if it ruins him"* and I found God calling me to do that (Psalm 15:4b Living Bible).

What Are We Teaching Our Boys?

When I was at Bezek Centre, my associate Garth Hunt had an after-school program for boys aged twelve to fifteen. On Thursdays, they would get off the school bus, have a game of touch football, a simple meal, and then a Bible study with a prayer time. Many of them became Christians.

We had other guests staying with us when the boys came. One woman asked me what we taught them. After my short explanation, she asked me, "Are you teaching these boys how to become good husbands and fathers?"

It brought me up short. I had to ask myself, "Are we?" We concluded that to be a good father, one first has to be a good son. We need to learn how to honour our father whether he is alive or not; whether he is an abusive drunk, an arrogant autocrat, or a caring parent. Some of us need memory healing about that relationship, for people most often reproduce what they have experienced. The way we lead in our family is often similar to what we saw when growing up (Titus 2:6-8).

Living with Compromise

It is very difficult to be a politician today. It's hard for members of Parliament to be forced to vote with the party when it goes against their convictions. But we are unfair if we criticize the one who cannot completely follow the Lord's agenda as she or he sits in the House of Commons or serves in politics at any level. Politics is the art of compromise without selling your soul. Sometimes one has to settle for half a loaf if the whole cannot be won. But there are times when men and women must declare themselves, even abandoning their political party if it requires them to deny their Lord and follow the ways of ungodliness. Most often, party leaders require conformity. In a Canadian parliamentary vote on same-sex marriage, members of the governing party were told that they could vote according to their consciences, except for cabinet members. They had to vote as they were told or forfeit their cabinet post. Sadly, only one cabinet minister resigned to vote against the legislation.

The Open and the Secret Life

One of the problems we all face is how to square our conduct with what is going on in our minds. Sometimes it is easier to do the right thing than to think the right thing. Paul speaks about taking every thought captive to obey Christ (2 Corinthians 1:5). One may be polite and be careful to fulfill every agreement with another person but despise her in one's heart. A woman may make a show of loyalty to her leader, but in her mind she is thinking of ways to undercut his authority and get rid of him. In one church where I was the pastor, some folks took strong opposition to my preaching about the necessity of the new birth (John 3:3). But those who were against me were open about it. I hated the conflict, but I was glad that there was no deception. We knew where we stood with each other.

Men, Women, and Lust

A snare for many men and women is how they look at women and men, especially ones they find attractive. One may act like a real gentleman when relating to a woman and at the same time may be lusting after her in his heart. And vice versa, though it may be less well-advertised that women face the same temptations. The contemporary world view has tried to normalize same-sex lust, also.

Lust is destructive to a person's soul, for it intends inequality and makes of the person lusted after a sex object rather than a person, beloved of God and intended for holiness. We need great grace as we wrestle to take captive lustful thoughts in order to become women and men of integrity. The devil is always encouraging us to secretly play his game of "vain imaginings" as he seeks to gain a foothold in our minds. The Psalmist was aware of this when he made this request to the Lord: *"Search me, O God, and know my heart! Try me and know my thoughts! And see if there be any wicked way in me, and lead me in the way everlasting!"* (Psalm 139:23-24). Jesus warned people to guard their eyes and thoughts.

A sermon preached nearly 200 years ago by the Rev. W. Robertson of Brighton, England, was entitled "The Expulsive Power of a New Affection." The main thrust of his sermon was this: "Loving Jesus more than the sinful fantasy will expel the fantasy. Loving Jesus more than the destructive habit will diminish its power." What you feed will grow. What you starve will wither. So, it's obvious: feed the virtue, starve the sin.

Sexuality and the Media

A report from a large stadium meeting of men, hosted by Promise Keepers, said that an invitation was given for any man to come down to the field in an act of repentance for sin. Thousands responded. The great majority of the men who did so came because of having difficulty with their thought lives in relation to lust. No surprises there!

James writes, *"Each person is tempted when he is lured and enticed by his own desire. Then desire when it has conceived gives birth to sin; and sin when it is full-grown brings forth death"* (James 1:14-15). Lust may not be fully conquered, but let no man think that this is simply a natural condition that men can let have its way. Each bout of temptation requires a decision whether to do battle against it with the Lord's help or give in to it.

Much of the blame for the decline in morality can be laid at the feet of the media. Sexual encounters usually are portrayed as taking place outside of marriage. Business morality is shown as "what you can get away with." The judiciary and the police often are shown to be "on the take," so mistrust of them is natural. It is a constant uphill struggle to convince our children that although this is what many people do, there are better ways, and then to teach and to live them.

Agnes Moyer spoke for many of us when, in the *Washington Post*, she described the film industry as "demonstrating a progressive vulgarization of public morals." Concerning television, a commentator wrote, "the networks are in a race to the bottom." Of course, those who produce the movies and the programming always say, "This is what the people want. If you don't want it, don't watch it." But it is difficult to escape.

A news report that a chain store in the United States had decided to select for sale only those videos that were "family friendly" was followed by another report that "Hollywood was outraged." Children are taught from an early age to take their cues from their peers in language, dress, and conduct rather than from responsible adults. Values are said to be only what you choose them to be. There's a cultural war going on, and we are not winning it yet.

Honouring the Bible

Integrity in the Christian faith requires honour for the Word of God. In many churches, the scriptures are given little place; the strong name of Jesus is largely unspoken in the sermon; the Holy Spirit uninvited. Seldom are heard Jesus' words, *"I am the way, and the truth, and the life; no one comes to the Father, but by me"* (John 14:6).

When I was ordained to the Christian ministry, I was asked by the ordaining officer this question:

> "Are you persuaded that the Holy Scriptures contain sufficiently all doctrines required for eternal salvation in our Lord Jesus Christ? And are you resolved out of the said Scriptures to instruct the people committed to your charge, and to teach nothing which is not agreeable thereto?"

The required answer was, "I am so persuaded, and am so resolved, by God's grace." That was my answer then, and five decades later, it remains the same. I don't understand every difficult passage, but I am willing to study it and struggle with it, and I am open to receive further light.

Commitment

A minister friend of mine told me that he had plans, hopes, and dreams for his church. Some of them were long range. He was disappointed because his board showed little enthusiasm for his ideas. Finally he asked one of the members why they were resistant to his proposals. The answer was, "You suggest projects that will take a number of years to complete. We don't know whether you will be here to help us carry them out."

My friend realized that he had made no commitment to stay

and work with his people to fulfill these hopes and dreams. He went to his board and said, "By God's grace I commit to stay as your pastor for the next five years." The board members quickly, and with enthusiasm, began planning to begin the projects that their pastor had proposed.

Integrity

Integrity means being faithful to God and His purposes; being faithful to our spouses, our children, and our aging parents. It means being loyal to the fellowship and giving honour to our leaders. I'm not suggesting that we who are being led should give unthinking obedience to our leaders. They, too, are fallible; however, we don't have to "yes but" their every decision.

We are to be good stewards of God's creation and to care for the poor and downtrodden. We have a responsibility to look after our own health. Jesus did say, *"My yoke is easy, and my burden is light"* (Matthew 11:30). So don't pick up more of a load than He gives you or let someone else insist on what your load is. God's burden for you is the right weight. Excess weight is somebody else's idea for us.

3

For the Flock:
Choosing Leaders

The Idea of Leadership

As St. Paul knew from his own efforts both to destroy and to build the new church, sound leadership is essential to a successful church—as it is to any organization. In the church, it is expected that leaders will be men and women of prayer and students of the Word. (Secular groups do not require this, but it wouldn't be a bad idea if some of them did.) The leader will provide good direction and godly motivation in an atmosphere where eagerness is appreciated and those being led feel secure. He will not avoid disciplining the unruly or cheering on the discouraged. Good leaders impart enthusiasm to their people. Such qualities in leadership are gifts of God.

But strangely, in some settings, there are those who don't like the idea of calling someone "leader." They say it makes one person "more important" than the others. While the ground is level at the foot of the Cross—all believers are equal in Christ—different gifts are granted to various people. When I have been invited to teach in a group, I want to know who is in charge. To my question "Who is your leader?" once in awhile I have found those who think it very spiritual to reply, "Oh, we don't have any particular leader; the Holy Spirit leads us. Nobody should tell someone else what to do. We are all equal here." This may *sound* spiritual but actually is unscriptural and unrealistic. Without a designated leader, even a simple thing like getting a meeting together is difficult. Without leadership, it's hard to begin or end a meeting. But far more important, without leadership, a vision or mission cannot be coordinated. Such a vision may not even exist. Someone has to lead.

The Problem of *Equal* Leadership

On the other hand, confusion is guaranteed when a congregation or other organization has several leaders all, supposedly, with the same level of authority. They are said to be *equal.* I quote from an advertisement in a church magazine:

> "To achieve our mission we are seeking an ordained person for the new full-time position of 'Minister of Children and Youth, Worship and Outreach.' The ideal candidate will work as an *equal team member* with our present full-time minister and other staff" (emphasis added).

What do they mean by equal? If each person's area of responsibility is clearly defined, things may go well, but when a major decision that will affect the whole organization is required, the word *equal* becomes a tricky word. There will be confusion and uncertainty over who makes the big decision. Who is the real captain of the team? If there is not one so designated, either there will be a failure to act or several of the "equals" will start jockeying for the reins. Christian people are supposed to be able to come to agreement regarding God's agenda for them. But the structure of most churches requires the expertise of a leader to know how to develop God's agenda within that structure. Someone must be legitimately identified as being "in charge." That leader is the one, who after consultation with the brothers and sisters, will say, "This is what we will do." Humility is important, but the idea of co-leadership seems to me to be a contradiction in terms.

Power Factions and Manipulative Strategies

Personal Agendas

If a group gathers to do business and an important issue is to be decided, someone with a personal agenda may invite a few cohorts to meet for coffee beforehand and arrange who will make the desired motion and who will second it. Then, in the meeting, with whispers and nudges, the usurper manipulates the gathering to subversive ends.

I have experienced this sort of dishonest manoeuvring in a particular church meeting where I was the chairman. The church board was meeting to discuss the renewal of the contract of a valued associate in ministry. I found out later that a small clique had met earlier and arranged that a motion not to renew her contract be made, but that it be voted on without discussion and by secret ballot. The way people would vote had been canvassed, and in very short order my colleague was gone. I had been blindsided.

Through planned politicking, a meeting can be swept into a move that people might not choose if all of the facts were out in the open and the matter fairly discussed. One who can pull this off may take pride in being the "real" power source and undercover leader. However, the opportunity for the body of Christ to become of one mind and spirit has been annihilated. The rule of order for a church board should not permit motions for action without discussion. The information we have about the early church members being *one in heart and mind*" (Acts 4:32 NIV) suggests a standard for getting to the bottom of our differences to find the will of God for us all.

In the above case, I knew who had arranged for the motions to be put forth as they were. He got his way that time by such means but never again. Throughout my ministry at that church, I was in conflict with that man. Our views regarding what church should be were very different.

Waiting Them Out

Such a clique can work in another way. I was told it used to happen in the old days of the Mine Mill and Smelter Workers Union meetings in Sudbury: a group with its own agenda might prolong the meeting with endless talk until most members grew weary and went home. The ones strongly committed to their agenda waited until the ranks had thinned to their liking, and then they put forth their motion. This patient, committed group considered themselves to have more wisdom than the larger assembly of union members. They chose this way of getting their way. They felt that they were the committed ones. I suppose that could be called a form of leadership, but again it represents the manipulation of the many by the few, not a coming together to find the common good or the will of God.

Weak Leaders

Too Tolerant Leaders

If a leader is too permissive, too fearful of offending anyone, there will be no direction or restraint in the meeting. In a fellowship of Christians, one troubled soul might babble on endlessly about his aches and pains, always asking to be the centre of attention; another will talk on and on about her latest revelations and dreams. A confident leader, however, can stop them. Authority is given from Above and acknowledged from below. Someone has said, "Authority is to society what gravity is to the universe. Without authority everything flies off in all directions and the people are divided, confused, defeated, and scattered." Every group needs leadership—called by God, agreed to by the people, accepted by the leader, and acknowledged by the overseer. Otherwise the group will go nowhere or just become mired in confusion.

The Wrong Leader

Some leaders are chosen by the vote of the people to be led; others are appointed by a higher outside authority. Sadly, choices may be influenced exclusively by a person's natural abilities rather than by an evaluation of her or his spiritual ones. In politics, it may be the one who has the most money and the best organization who wins. But in churches, too, we sometimes pick one who is not God's choice.

The prophet Hosea noticed this when he wrote, *"Like people, like priest"* (Hosea 4:9). We might reverse the order and say, "Like priest, like people." People will begin to think and act like their leader. If the leader is off track, then the group may miss the way as well. It's difficult to correct her or remove him from office because many assume the leader is right or will have been convinced that is so.

Worldly Qualifications

It's not wise to elect someone as leader just because that person has a high profile in the community. But that should not disqualify the person either. Paul says in his letter: "I want you to appoint elders in every town who are well thought of for their good lives. They must have only one wife and their children must love the Lord and not have a reputation for being disobedient to their parents" (Titus 1:5-6 author's paraphrase). We have to look at this in a way that does not disqualify everyone as a candidate. Nobody is perfect nor can one guarantee that his children will always behave well. Many great leaders in Israel such as Samuel, David, Eli, and Solomon had very difficult and rebellious sons. We don't know whether Paul had children or not, but in his letter, he sets out the ideal and trusts that leaders will grow towards meeting that ideal. Some Christians feel justified in placing unreasonable or even cruel expectations upon their children because they want their family to appear exemplary.

This has been a recurring problem in the church. We must accept the truth that we and our families are works in progress.

Important Qualities

Delegating Responsibility

Different structures evolve in groups according to local needs. Some systems work better than others. But no matter what the structure, when people know what is expected of them, there is likely to be peace. Otherwise, they will fall over one another trying to do the same job while other tasks may not get done at all. For the group to function smoothly, individuals should know "who is responsible for what." It should be settled early, and it can be adjusted as you see what works.

A leader might say something like the following:

"Caroline, how about coming to the next meeting prepared to lead a discussion on tithing."

"Ray, will you arrange some refreshments for the next meeting and set up a roster of those who will provide refreshments for the five gatherings after that?"

"We are getting to the place where we need a building of our own. Charlie, you've had some building experience, will you head up a little study group with Joan and Andrew and bring us a report in three weeks with some recommendations?"

Reachable Standards

When Paul, in discussing leaders, wrote that they should *"be blameless"* (Titus 1:6), he was setting a standard that, of course, could be interpreted as impossible to meet. Jesus is the only one who is blameless. Yet, we are called to be like Him. But the old sinful nature continues to show its face from time to time and each of us could disqualify himself from ever holding any office in the church. Paul is rightly concerned that a leader should not be in the courts suing her Christian brother over some property line or financial matter. He should not be known to brawl in the streets or beat his wife, but be seen to live a life without public blame.

This does not mean he or she may abuse their children in private or engage in secret vices. And if we want our children to become faithful adults, then we had better not get so busy with church or business that we don't take the time to give them love and instruction. We are to be growing in grace, increasingly showing the fruit of the Spirit as we mature in our Christian walk. In short, a leader should give some evidence of Christian faith to unbelievers.

The Humility for Check-ups

Paul was concerned that whether we are leaders or the led, we don't become careless in our walk with the Lord. He wrote, *"Examine yourselves, to see whether you are holding to your faith. Test yourselves"* (2 Corinthians 13:5). It is vital that, from time to time, we assess where we are going. There are also times when we need a mentor who will help us become disciplined in our prayer and study life, someone who will challenge us as to whether we are giving quality time to our spouse and our children.

I remember a time in my early ministry when our family's finances were in chaos. My wife and I swallowed our pride and asked a brother minister to sit down with us and show us how we could get hold of our spending and live within our means. We were grateful, but pride almost kept us from asking for help. So we thank God for His provision of leaders, mentors, counsellors, and companions. They are His gifts to us.

4

Leading People, Their Things, and Their Money

The Pushers and Butters

Dealing with difficult people nose to nose is something every leader faces. Opinionated, obstreperous, bullying, and nasty people were in the churches on Crete; they are with us today. Ezekiel (34:21-22 NIV) prophesied against such people:

Because you shove with flank and shoulder, butting all the weak sheep with your horns until you have driven them away, I will save my flock, and they will no longer be plundered. I will judge between one sheep and another.

For some sheep, every leadership decision arouses a protest. *"For there are many rebellious people, mere talkers and deceivers, especially those of the circumcision group"* (Titus 1:10 NIV). Some will tell you that they know a better way of doing things than you do. Others will say that the old ways were best and imply that nothing should ever be done for the first time. A person might insist that the Lord has spoken to him about a decision you made that was wrong. He will try to buttress his case by using spiritual additives such as, "While I was praying, the Lord told me...." We expect our people to pray, but they should not insist that because they pray a lot, they have an open and exclusive hotline to Heaven or that they know better than the leader what should be done. This is spiritual manipulation. If somebody gets some light from praying, she or he may share it with the leader and then leave it with him to consider. The leader must consider it prayerfully and act on it or not.

Don't Abdicate Your Calling

Perhaps you, the leader, have not done much praying lately. You may feel particularly unspiritual and wonder if you are really fit to lead. Circumstances may have caused you to be a bit depressed. Don't yield to the temptation to abdicate your God-given role by "coming under" someone who seems much more spiritual than you do. There are those who would like to bring you into subjection and defraud you of your calling. Paul said that some *"must be silenced"* (Titus 1:11 NIV).

On the other hand, it can be a good thing when someone offers some insight, perhaps a word of knowledge or wisdom, which will be exactly what you need. It takes a measure of humility on your part to receive it and wisdom enough to know that this does not make you any less a leader. In the church, as in business, the leader does not have to know everything; he just has to know who can provide it for him. Don't be afraid to ask someone for information or insight who has a better take on a situation than you do. Light can come from many sources, and God will give you discernment to test the input you receive.

Getting People To Share Their Insights

Someone may receive godly insight for the church but from feelings of inadequacy or shyness thinks it would be presumptuous to give it to you, the leader. We need to create a climate of security among our people to make them feel comfortable in coming to us by encouraging them to share the good things that God has been showing them. A mature leader will have a welcoming spirit but know how to rebuke lovingly the bore and the time waster. We were always taught that it was proper etiquette for the one who initiates a phone call also to end it. But there are times when we need to say gently, "I think we've covered the matter. We'll talk again. Goodbye." There will be times when someone who has come for counsel or just a visit has overstayed his or her welcome. You can say, with a smile, "I'm throwing you out now." Such a dismissal is not lacking in love; it is simply one way of ending communication that has already been completed.

Stewardship...

Of the House of God

Paul says that we are to be blameless as stewards of God (Titus 1:7). A steward is one who manages someone else's property. The Psalmist says, *"The earth is the Lord's and the fulness thereof, the world and those who dwell therein"* (Psalm 24:1). We are to treat His creation well without worshiping it. A man can mess up his corner of creation so easily. Christians are not blameless here. I have seen a church property with litter in the parking lot, paint peeling from the church's window frames, and last Sunday's sermon title still on the outdoor sign. On entering, I found that the place needed a good tidying and there was little that was attractive to the eye. The bulletin board was advertising events long past. I felt that these were reflections of their poor spiritual condition and leadership that was not alert. A good steward will not allow those seemingly minor things to gives the premises a look of being uncared for.

Of Money

Because God's people give money for the Lord's work, someone has to make sure it is handled properly. Early in my ministry, I became pastor of a small new church. We met in borrowed premises. The offering was being handled by one man. I was never able to pin him down, but what he reported in the offering seemed less than what I thought it should be. I believe he was skimming. He protested when I asked that two people count the weekly offering. To avoid suspicion or embarrassment, at least two people should handle church funds and report the amounts to the appropriate committee. The people should be confident that their money is handled well.

> For the grace of God that brings salvation has appeared to all men. It teaches us to say "No" to ungodliness and worldly passions, and to live self-controlled, upright and godly lives in this present age (Titus 2:11-12 NIV).

Of the Greater Treasures

Stewards of God are responsible for sharing the Word of God and the spiritual treasures in it. We are called to love the scriptures and be eager to explore their depths and then teach about them. We have a generous Father who is pleased to share the riches of His Kingdom, but they are not always easy to find.

We must search for them, dig them out, and bring them to our people. This takes time, effort, and patience.

Many Christians are biblically illiterate and content to be so. We need to encourage our people to do some digging on their own. Paul told his young friend Timothy, *"Do your best to present yourself to God as one approved, a workman who does not need to be ashamed and who correctly handles the word of truth"* (2 Timothy 2:15 NIV). Paul is saying the same thing to us. A people who are studying the Word of God likely will become more faithful disciples of Jesus.

Of the Flock

A good steward is wise enough to know that although he may have access to all the treasures of his master's household, they do not belong to him. But he is to care for them as though they were his own. A pastor may speak of "My people" or "My church," but they are not his, except to look after. He is the shepherd who cares for the Master's sheep. The prophet Ezekiel refers to some shepherds who were responsible for looking after God's people but were poor stewards. So, this is what the Lord God said:

> Woe to the shepherds of Israel who only take care of themselves!...[Y]ou do not take care of the flock. You have not strengthened the weak or healed the sick or bound up the injured. You have not brought back the strays or searched for the lost. You have ruled them harshly and brutally...I will hold them accountable (Ezekiel 34:2-4,10 NIV).

Greedy and Uncaring Shepherds

The prophet Ezekiel tells us plainly that we are not to be like those shepherds. Through the prophet the Lord God complains that some of these men were in the ministry to enrich themselves. We must not be among them who are in it for the "filthy lucre." If you have a church credit card, be ruthless in discerning what is for the church and don't use it for anything else. If you are getting paid for mileage, be scrupulous in recording it accurately.

Ezekiel says, *"You have not brought back the strays."* We recognize that some who were once part of the fellowship have drifted away, and we have not gone after them. And we are only too aware that many in our own neighbourhood have not yet received a gracious invitation to become a part of the family of God.

Seeking the Lost...

Robert Walmsley's old hymn, "Come Let Us Sing of a Wonderful Love" has a beautiful line, "Seeking the lost, seeking the lost; saving, redeeming at measureless cost." We are to encourage our people to search for the lost and bring them in. We make them welcome, and Jesus does the saving and redeeming. We draw them, as they are ready, into the life of the fellowship. Our Lord has a deep interest in each one. Do we reflect His interest?

...with Jesus

We can too easily come to the conclusion that leading is just too heavy a task. Yes, it is. That is why Jesus said, *"Without Me you can do nothing"* (John 15:5 NKJV). Or, "Without Me, you can do nothing that is of eternal consequence." In 2 Corinthians 12:9, Paul spoke of Christ's great promise to all, including those who are called to leadership, *"My grace is sufficient for you, for my power is made perfect in weakness."* That is great news.

Every leader does well also to have some solid human support from colleagues who know and understand her or his burden. The leader also needs to help equip each Christian to be able to graciously share the faith, not just leaving it up to the professional.

The New Church

The new converts *"devoted themselves to the apostles' teaching and fellowship, to the breaking of bread and the prayers"* (Acts 2:42). That model is good for us, also, as we study the scriptures, share meals sometimes, including the Lord's Supper, and learn to pray both individually and in groups. We also have good fellowship, which includes having fun together as God's people. We want to see our church become family, but we don't want to become ingrown, either. We are to keep our hearts open to those who need what we ourselves are finding in Jesus.

The Task and the Reward

St. Paul (Titus 3:3-9 NIV) writes,

At one time we too were foolish, disobedient, deceived and enslaved by all kinds of passions and pleasures. We lived in malice and envy, being hated and hating one another. But when the kindness and love of God our Saviour appeared, he saved us, not because of righteous things we had done, but because of his mercy. He saved us through the washing of rebirth and renewal by the Holy Spirit, whom he poured out on us generously through Jesus Christ our Saviour, so that, having been justified by his grace, we might become heirs having the hope of eternal life. This is a trustworthy saying. And I want you to stress these things, so that those who have trusted in God may be careful to devote themselves to doing what is good. These things are excellent and profitable for everyone.

5

For the Flock: Disqualify or Redeem a Leader?

Bad Leaders

Paul uses the major part of his letter to Titus to discuss character in church leaders. He is deeply concerned about quality leadership in the church because leaders affect not only what goes on inside the fellowship but are often the human face of Christianity that the townsfolk see. What they see and hear about the leaders certainly influences any decision they make about whether or not to join that people. Paul writes (Titus 1:7) concerning the things he looks for in a leader:

1. Not self-willed;
2. Not quick to anger;
3. Not a heavy drinker;
4. Not violent;
5. Not greedy or pursuing dishonest gain.

These are the characteristics under scrutiny.

Renovations or Removals

Apparently some of the Cretans in the churches, including their leaders, came out of pretty rough backgrounds and needed not only outward polishing, but some radical inner changes in their lives. Paul frankly acknowledges what he and other converts were like before encountering Jesus: *"At one time we too were foolish, disobedient, deceived and enslaved by all kinds of passions and pleasures. We lived in malice and envy, being hated and hating one another"* (Titus 3:3 NIV). Some of them had their own ungodly agendas:

For there are many rebellious people, mere talkers and deceivers, especially those of the circumcision group. They must be silenced, because they are ruining whole households by teaching things they ought not to teach—and that for the sake of dishonest gain (Titus 1:10-11 NIV).

Before Paul ends his letter he says again:

But avoid foolish controversies and genealogies and arguments and quarrels about the law, because these are unprofitable and useless. Warn a divisive person once, and then warn him a second time. After that, have nothing to do with him (Titus 3:9-10).

In a congregation I once served, a man started to worship with us and immediately set about trying to introduce New Age ideas to our people. He, along with a few like-minded other men and women he brought in, tried to get elected to the eldership. Our people were aware that there was something wrong with their beliefs and values. When he failed to get himself and his little clique elected, they angrily left. That experience caused us to re-examine our own beliefs. We are not to be closed to new ideas, but we need to be alert to that which would erode and destroy the biblical faith.

Learning to Serve

In 1929, a Canadian preacher named Wallace Hamilton developed one of the first drive-in churches in America. It was located near St. Petersburg, Florida. For forty years, over 10,000 people gathered each Sunday in their cars to hear him preach in what was once a wasteland abandoned from the Florida land bust of the late 1920s. I heard him preach once in a Toronto church and was so impressed that out of my meagre student resources, I bought one of his books, *Ride the Wild Horses*, subtitled "The Christian Use of Our Untamed Impulses." Some of his insights, which I use here, helped me to see how negatives in some leaders can be turned into positives.

Consider the self-willed, arrogant, and ambitious man. Such a man is certain of his opinions and may lead, but he does so by bullying and manipulating his followers. He has a huge ego and is always looking for ways in which he can be honoured. He wants to make things happen, but on his terms. But God can see in him the man he might become if he humbles himself and admits that his role and standing in the Kingdom are what God gives him—not what he assumes for himself. He needs to learn to serve well before he can lead well. Moses found this out when he murdered an Egyptian taskmaster in an abortive attempt to rescue the enslaved Israelites from the hand of Pharaoh. He had to learn to do things God's way. He found that it required herding sheep for forty years in the wilderness before he was able to hear God speak to him about how His mission was to be carried out.

Seeking Excellence

Lest we lose the good parts of these seemingly negative characteristics in a man or woman—arrogance, ambition, and self-will—we might rather recognize that they contain the seeds of the desire to excel. We are not called to be flat-lined people who have no opinion, no fire, no ambition. There isn't necessarily a huge gap between a man who wants to be important and a man who wants to do great things for God; between a woman wanting to impress and a woman who wants to excel in moral greatness and service to the Kingdom. When we read the prayer of Jabez (1 Chronicles 4:9), we hear the cry of a man wanting a larger ministry for God's sake, not his own. So we must not stifle that part of the person who can be directed to want to accomplish great things for God. Let ambition be for the sake of the Gospel. The good leader looks for ways to harness that ambition for the Kingdom.

Angry for a Purpose

Paul lists the next fault: "Quick to anger." That's a person who has a short fuse. Many people hide their anger well. They seethe within over real or imagined hurts. Such people might control their rage for years and then suddenly explode, creating havoc. Others who are continuously angry often make no apology for it. One will say, "My mother was always angry about something. I inherited my nature from her. So what do you expect?" It is one thing to have a predisposition to a certain characteristic but it's another thing to take ancestral pride in it.

If an angry person is the leader, she will leave anxious and wounded followers in her wake. Such a woman needs to be brought to her knees before the Cross and the anger turned against the wickedness of the world. It's not easy to confront an angry man and suggest he take an anger-management course, but if he continues unchanged, he will destroy the joy of those around him. It may be even harder to confront a woman whose anger has become bitterness shrouded in layers of rationalization, but such a woman cannot discern truth to minister in power.

Prevention and Healing

Dietrich Bonhoeffer wrote, "Christians have as much a duty to remove a drunk driver from a car as to attend to those he has run over." One knows how offended a person is who has had too much to drink when a friend wants to take away the car keys and order a taxi. There is a time for removing a destructive leader as well as for tending to those he or she has wounded.

We Need Fighters

The capacity for intense feeling is one of those characteristics that can be used to seek justice. Who should not be angry at the child pornography that floods the Internet? Who should simply shrug when he sees the government's ever-expanding building and promotion of gambling casinos and the havoc they create? Who does not weep over the increasing number of people living on the streets? Who would not be saddened and angry at the common use of alcohol and drugs at high school proms and the teenage pregnancies and abortions that are often the result of their use?

Well-directed anger is a quality Jesus exercised as He drove the money changers from the temple or blistered the religious leadership of His day, calling them *"whited sepulchres...full of dead men's bones"* (Matthew 23:27 KJV). Saul was a man of temper when he attacked and persecuted Christians, but when he was converted and renamed Paul, he did not lose his fighting spirit but became a soldier for Christ. He declared at the end of his life, *"I have fought the good fight, I have finished the race, I have kept the faith"* (2 Timothy 4:7). His metaphors are intense. A person who cannot become angry to the point of doing something about sin, poverty, and injustice is a person who lacks moral indignation and courage. I remember hearing of one author who thanked his political opponents for keeping him angry enough to complete his book! But that anger should not rule the person's spirit or cloud the judgment.

The Misuse of Alcohol

The third characteristic noted in Paul's short list is the misuse of alcohol. There are some churches where abstinence is a prerequisite for membership. Other churches may use wine in Communion. Many use unfermented grape juice or offer a choice. Temperance was a major topic of sermons in times past. Not so now. Some churches provide an open bar at social functions. Paul does not condemn the use of alcohol, but he says being a heavy drinker is not good for a leader. It leads to loss of objectivity, vision, and memory. It is difficult to respect a leader who may show up at a meeting slurring words and walking with uncertain gait, pretending to be perfectly in control.

Many people drink alcohol to excess because they are trying to cover up some pain or loss. Some, wanting to fit in, start drinking and become addicted. Heavy drinking is sometimes a symptom of despair concerning the future. Many churches are pleased to share their facilities with AA groups, which specialize in helping men and women to become sober.

Proper Thirst

The man with a great thirst for alcohol is the man who, when his heart has been turned to God, turns his thirst for booze into a thirst for God Himself. Jesus said, *"Blessed are those who hunger and thirst for righteousness, for they shall be satisfied"* (Matthew 5:6). Again He said, *"If any one thirst, let him come to me and drink. He who believes in me, as the scripture has said, 'Out of his heart shall flow rivers of living water'"* (John 7:37-38). Paul said, *"And do not get drunk with wine, for that is debauchery; but be filled with the Spirit"* (Ephesians 5:18).

People of all ages take drugs or drink alcohol in the beginning because they want to belong; they want to be "cool." Many feel unloved and see no hopeful future for themselves. Alcohol or drugs will temporarily dull the pain, but the hangover will just bring deeper frustration and despair. Love and acceptance, along with some open doors that lead to finding purpose in life, will bring changes in the appetite and a lessening desire for artificial stimulants. This change, however, requires a major investment in love, patience, wisdom, and time from pastors, fellow addicts committed to sobriety, and understanding members of the church.

Manipulations of the Violent

Paul goes on to mention violence as a character trait that is unacceptable in any leader. Violence can destroy a home. That is why we have safe houses for women who have fled, with their children, from terrifying home situations. So much pain is caused when the strong intimidate the weak. But violence is not an expression of strength; it is the weapon of those who are trying to be powerful because they actually are insecure. They wound and destroy those around them in a pitiful attempt to prove themselves superior to others. Verbal abuse, which is a frequently overlooked form of violence, can be threatening in itself but often is combined with actual violence or with the threat of violence. Alcohol plays a role here, frequently, by loosening the self-control of the deeply wounded and unhealed spirit. As Paul observes, *"At one time we too were foolish, disobedient, deceived and enslaved by all kinds of passions and pleasures. We lived in malice and envy, being hated and hating one another"* (Titus 3:3 NIV) Evidently, Paul himself was a violent man.

These days we hear of "Toxic Ministries." Some ministers may appear to be successful, but they operate with "soul force" to bring about what, for a season, seems like success. When they are confronted they show no humility, just violence. If men can appear threatening, women also can be abusive, but more usually with their tongues. A violent board member intimidates people into capitulating to her own way. They fear that if things do not go as she wishes, she will lose her temper and tear the meeting apart. Such an obnoxious person, whether woman or man, is not fit to be a leader in the church nor even a member of the board, for he or she will become hostile with those who disagree with the favoured point of view. I have known such persons on my church boards. There is bottled-up energy there that, when wrongly released, creates havoc.

Explosives Turned to Good Use.

Lest we abandon all hope for a violent person, we should remember that the dynamite that can blow up a perfectly good bridge can also be used to uproot stumps to make way for a farm. Log-runs in rivers often were troubled by log jams. They caused those rivers to overflow and flood the surrounding area. Then, a man who knew what he was doing would carefully put a stick of dynamite in the right place. The explosion would loosen the whole jam so the logs could move again down the river to the mill, ending the flood.

Sometimes a situation that is holding up the progress of the church's work requires a person's exploding over something to get things going again. It must be for God's purposes, however, not the unrestrained temper of a person who, if he or she does not get his or her own way, threatens to destroy the peace of the church. There is a place for righteous anger; no place for violence. Self-control is a fruit of the Spirit. *"Rather he must be...one...who is self-controlled, upright, holy, and disciplined"* (Titus 1:8 NIV).

Dishonest Gain

The last in Paul's list is the greedy man. Some are in the Lord's work for their own gain. Peter writes, *"Tend the flock of God that is your charge, not by constraint but willingly, not for shameful gain but eagerly"* (1 Peter 5:2-3). The term "shameful gain" is elsewhere translated as "filthy lucre."

One night I attended a church where an evangelistic service was being held. After the meeting was over, I went looking for the washroom. Not sure where I was going, I approached an area where the church offices were located. I heard loud voices coming from the pastor's office. The visiting evangelist and the pastor of the church were arguing over the division of the offering. The evangelist wanted more than the pastor wanted to give him. Voices were raised in anger, and the language was unseemly. What a sad footnote to an evening at which a number of people confessed faith in Christ.

Our culture conditions us to always want more, and that plague is no respecter of persons. Whether in the Lord's work or in a business, working for oneself or as a member of a union, a person's eyes should not always be on how to get more money. Jesus asked *"What shall it profit a man, if he gain the whole world, and lose his own soul?"* (Mark 8:36 KJV). A man's greed is to be transformed into a desire for a bigger outreach, more people reached with the Gospel and won for God's Kingdom.

Invest Rather Than Discard

How much better that a Christian's destructive tendencies be directed into useful paths for the Kingdom than to discard the person as unfit to serve as a Christian leader. Changes to the inner being are never easy or simple, but God is in the business of redeeming and changing men and women. Jesus said, *"Him that cometh to me I will in no wise cast out"* (John 6:37 KJV). We should not intend just to get rid of leaders and officials who create trouble in the church; it's just that such people should not be allowed to control things until their negative strengths have been transformed into positive ones. This requires the investment of men in oversight positions who are not afraid to confront the troubled one and offer counsel. Those who are in charge, therefore, must themselves be good examples of principled leadership.

6

Teach Sound Doctrine

Why Doctrine Is Important

Paul, in his letter to Titus, said, *"Teach what befits sound doctrine"* (Titus 2:1). Some people base their beliefs on prejudiced misinformation. God wants a people whose thoughts, words, and actions are authored by the Spirit of Jesus Christ. From the Bible, we learn how we can become that kind of people. Wondering about what God has done, what He is doing, how He relates to the universe, and how we understand these things brings us to the study of Christian doctrine. We don't use the word *doctrine* much in conversation, but a Christian doctrine is a foundational truth that when connected to other such truths comprises the body of Christian belief and practice.

The belief system of many people is based on a collection of shallow or transitory religious opinions. If your group wants to operate on a solid foundation, learning the essential truths of the Christian faith is necessary. Studying doctrine is not a matter of doing dry theological gymnastics. Like some science, it is a laboratory discipline that requires the testing and evaluating through experience of the principles set out in the Bible; it is learning and putting into practice those holy truths that make sense of God's world and our place in it. Gathering these good things about God and seeing them fit together helps us to know what He is like and how He relates to us.

If you connect these biblical truths or doctrines, they become like the vertebrae of a person's body. In a human body, the bones of the vertebrae, properly joined together, enable the body to stand up. Without the properly connected vertebrae, the rest of the human body would be a puddle of organs, muscles and bones; a skin full of unsavoury stew. So, with the backbone of sound doctrine, we are able to stand in our faith, stand up for our faith, and—as Paul says about fidelity to Christ—having done all still to stand (Ephesians 6:13).

Paul's three words *teach*, *sound*, and *doctrine* are verb, adjective, and noun.

1. We *teach* about God and His Christ.

2. We keep it *sound*: "based on well-grounded principles" (*Canadian Oxford Dictionary*).

3. We teach Christian *doctrine*: the truth about God and His plan for the human race affirmed by Jesus that has been proven from generation to generation.

Condensations of the Christian Faith

Over the centuries, there have been noble attempts to hammer out, in condensed form, the essence of the Christian faith. The Nicene Creed, the Apostle's Creed, and the Athanasian Creed, all written in the fourth and fifth centuries, try to encapsulate the major events in God's dealing with His creation. Later, various branches of the church brought forth statements containing the doctrines they believe and practices they ask their members to follow. Martin Luther, taking a stand against Rome, nailed his ninety-five theses to the Castle Church door at Wittenberg in 1523. The Anglicans gathered "Thirty Nine Articles" of doctrine in 1571, and shortly after that, the reformed churches wrote the

"Canons of Dort" (Dutch), the "Heidelberg Catechism" (German), and the "Belgic Confession" (Belgian). The Presbyterians proclaimed, as their doctrinal standard, the "Westminster Confession" (1690), and John Wesley, in the eighteenth century, left to the Methodists and posterity his "Doctrinal Standards." In 1925, the newly forming United Church of Canada presented the "Twenty Articles of the Basis of Union." Various other groups have written their own statements of faith. Some denominations continue to update their doctrinal statements of faith and write new creeds.

Paul's Blend of Belief and Ethics

For Paul, belief and morality are not to be separated. Wanting to avoid any imbalance of emphasis, in his letter to Titus he offers, in one sentence, an example of doctrine blended with a call to godly behaviour. He writes,

> *For the grace of God has appeared for the salvation of all men,* [doctrine] *training us to renounce irreligion and worldly passions, and to live sober, upright, and godly lives in this world,* [ethics] *awaiting our blessed hope, the appearing of the glory of our great God and Saviour Jesus Christ, who gave himself for us to redeem us from all iniquity and to purify for himself a people of his own who are zealous for good deeds* (Titus 2:11-14 emphasis added).

He adds, *"Declare these things"* (Titus 2:15).

Doctrines Come from God's Story

God's story is found in the Jewish and the Christian scriptures. It begins with Creation. Our spiritual ancestors Adam and Eve started well but, yielding to temptation and pride, rebelled against God's instructions and were ejected from Eden. This story provides the doctrine called "The Fall." Later, God called Abraham to be the first of the Patriarchs—the father of a nation. His grandson Jacob (renamed Israel) had twelve sons who became the heads of the twelve tribes of Israel. These Israelites, whom God called His own people, became enslaved in Egypt. God conscripted Moses to lead them out. God gave them the Ten Commandments and brought them into their own Promised Land.

Then came a parade of judges, kings, and prophets. God, speaking through the prophets, promised to the world a Messiah who would deliver His people from their sins.

Jesus was born and angels heralded His birth. At about age thirty, Jesus began preaching the Kingdom of God. He healed the sick, cast out demons, raised the dead, and so infuriated the religious hierarchy by His claims to be God's Son that they convinced the Romans to put Him to death. He was crucified, died, and was buried. On the third day, Jesus was raised from the dead; and by the Holy Spirit of the risen Christ, the church was gathered.

Jesus' death, resurrection, and ascension are the central events of the church's ongoing life and are celebrated as such. After Jesus ascended to heaven, the Holy Spirit was poured out, empowering the church to proclaim the Gospel to the world. Over time, the New Testament was written. The rest of the story is in the ongoing acts of the Holy Spirit in the lives of those who don't merely know stories about Jesus, they know Him.

Titus's Doctrines

Titus didn't have the New Testament to work with, but as someone St. Paul called "my true son in our common faith" (Titus 1:4), he must have heard as much or more from Paul about Jesus than we now possess in the New Testament. From the story of Jesus' life and death and resurrection come the doctrines of the Christian faith.

Paul also was well qualified to teach Titus the Jewish experience of God's dealing with His chosen people. From the disobedience of our spiritual ancestors comes the doctrine of sin—sin, which, as we well know, taints the whole human race. Man tried by many means to escape the guilt of sin. At first, people thought God demanded human sacrifice, but through Abraham they learned that animal's death was sufficient sign of a person's repentance (Genesis 22:8-13). Thus, in ancient Israel, animals were killed and their blood was sprinkled on the altar as a sign of contrition and to cleanse those who were penitent. The blood was believed to wash the sinner clean.

When Jesus appeared, He was recognized by the prophet John the Baptist as *"the Lamb of God, who takes away the sin of the world"* (John 1:29). Jesus fulfilled this role by obeying His Father God, even to the point of allowing His own blood to be shed. This doctrine we call the Atonement.

The ancient Jews had the idea that the more perfect the sacrificial animals, the more effective the restoration of their relationship with God; therefore, a lamb for sacrifice was to be "without spot or blemish." Jesus, Son of God and Son of Man, lived a sinless life. He made these astonishing claims for Himself: He allowed Himself to be called the *"Messiah, the Son of the living God"* (Matthew 16:16 The Message). He boldly declared *"He who has seen me has seen the Father"* (John 14:9). He said, *"No one comes to the Father, but by me"* (John 14:6) and performed amazing miracles, all of which led people to see Him as "a lamb without spot or blemish," a fitting sacrifice for the sins of the whole world. Those of us who recognize our own sins can see that we are just like those who conspired in killing Him, but He rose from the dead—demonstrating both the validity of His own prophecies and the truth that a person's spirit is not permanently connected to his or her flesh, but survives death. Jesus returned to the Father, to His God and our God, and is alive forever. He saves us from our sins and from eternal death, and His Spirit lives in those who welcome and trust Him. Titus knew the story of Jesus, and he surely taught its great truths—its doctrines.

We Also Teach Doctrine

Where does one start? Perhaps we begin with an event in Jerusalem on the day of Pentecost when God's Holy Spirit was poured out on 120 followers of Jesus who had gathered in an upper room. They burst out of that room into the street, and the commotion caused a great crowd of pilgrims to gather. Peter, the acknowledged leader, began to preach to the people in the street. He started talking about Jesus,

> *a man accredited by God to you by miracles, wonders and signs, which God did among you through him, as you yourselves know. This man was handed over to you by God's set purpose and foreknowledge; and you, with the help of wicked men, put him to death by nailing him to the cross. But God raised him from the dead, freeing him from the agony of death, because it was impossible for death to keep its hold on him"* (Acts 2:22-24).

When he finished his sermon, the crowd, convicted of sin, asked, *"What shall we do?"* Peter replied, *"Repent, and be baptized every one of you in the name of Jesus Christ for the forgiveness of your sins; and you shall receive the gift of the Holy Spirit"* (Acts 2:37-38). From this very condensed telling of the story, we develop doctrines of the faith: conviction of sin, repentance, forgiveness, the new birth, Christian baptism, and receiving the Holy Spirit, who brings the new life in Christ.

Thus was the church established, and over the years it spread and grew. It splintered, stumbled, became renewed, battled heresies, and passed through dark and dry times as well as revivals.

Through two millennia, the story of Jesus continues to be told and in the telling, the doctrines of the church are affirmed. People believe and learn to trust Jesus and begin the Christian life.

The New Life

Although beginning the Christian life is a "solo act," it makes us part of the Communion of Saints worldwide and heaven-wide. Locally, we are to be a part of a worshiping company of people who believe the same basic things about God but are able to accommodate most reasonable differences. Growing in this new life is a process of "applying the cross"; in other words, giving up the desires of our old nature and claiming the help of the Holy Spirit to develop our new nature. Paul writes, *"If any one is in Christ, he is a new creation; the old has passed away, behold, the new has come"* (2 Corinthians 5:17).

We are expected to grow towards maturity, and as we tell our story, others may want to know Jesus too. I once spoke to a group of people just before Christmas. We had sung the Christmas carol, "Hark the Herald Angels Sing" with its lines "Veiled in flesh the Godhead, see; Hail the incarnate Deity." I talked about the carol, about the loving invasion of God into His world through the birth of Christ. I spoke about the doctrine we call the Incarnation: that Jesus is God with us. He is the One who died for us and rose again. Later, over coffee, a woman said to me, "I brought a friend who was not a Christian. She said to me, 'When that fellow explained about the Incarnation, who Jesus is and what He did for us, it made sense. I have just now become a Christian.' She had to leave before coffee but she wanted you to know." Telling the story of Jesus can bring new life.

The Dreadful Part of the Story

A doctrine that is distressing to many is the doctrine of the Judgement. Many assume that everybody, when death comes, goes

61

to heaven. But the scriptures do not say that. The Bible verse many of us learned in Sunday school spells it out: *"God so loved the world that he gave his only begotten Son, that whosoever believeth in him should not perish, but have everlasting life"* (John 3:16 KJV). We don't presume to know the destiny of those who have never heard of Jesus, but those who have heard His gracious invitation to believe and have refused it are heading into the darkness according to their own choice.

A friend asked Henry David Thoreau, author and philosopher, what he thought of the world to come. He answered, "One world at a time, Chauncey, one world at a time." But the decision about the next world must be made in this world and while we have time. It's not God's will that any should miss heaven.

Years ago, Dr. Pusey of Oxford wrote, "None will be lost whom God can save without destroying in them His own gift of free will." This situation lends urgency to our roles as ambassadors of Christ.

We Can Do It

We are to live as people whose conduct and speech befits "sound doctrine" (1 Timothy 1:10). What we believe affects how we live.

We are not all preachers, teachers, or leaders in the church, but if we are part of God's people, we have our story to tell. We also have *The* Story to tell. It sounds a little heavy to expect that we should all stand on soap boxes and "teach sound doctrine," but we can share what we know and live out what we have experienced.

7

Where Leaders and Flock Go Astray

Conflicts for Titus

Paul wrote about problems with those of "the circumcision party" (Titus 1:10). They were sometimes called "Judaizers." They believed and pressured others to believe that to be a real Christian one must not only believe in Jesus as Messiah but also practice the whole of the Jewish law, which included dietary, ceremonial, and sabbath practices. Paul wrote that *"They must be silenced, since they are upsetting whole families by teaching for base gain what they have no right to teach"*(Titus 1:11). They confused new believers and were a nuisance to Paul. By saying "no" to their add-ons, he was trying to lighten the load of rule-bound Jews who had become believers in Jesus. He was also helping new Gentile believers escape being weighed down by the burden of trying to keep all the Jewish law.

Conflicts Today

A wounded Christian leader once said, "He who would lead the flock must fight the wolf." The leader in any setting where progress is being made must be prepared to face opposition, sometimes openly vicious, sometimes subtle; some from outside but often from inside the fellowship. The church is not free from politics, and politics has to do with "getting what we want." If it's government politics, it's "getting into and staying in power." If it's in the church, it's dealing with the ones who herd the "sacred cows."

Paul had a lot to say about people whose understanding of the content and practice of the faith differed from his. He tangled with people who had opposing agendas. Listen to what he had to put up with and think about what or who harasses us in the church today. Think how your group may be being affected by the introduction of heresies or by people stirring up dissension.

This idea should not seem strange to us because today we find people and groups who say that certain practices identify a person as a "good" Christian. The "Judaizers" are among us today trying to put loads on Christians that Jesus never intended. I heard one pastor say to some of his people, "Every time the church door is open, you should be there." He was in bondage to the institution and tried to enslave his people as well.

Some groups forbid their people to attend movies and dances. They forbid wearing lipstick or playing bridge. Some will not allow TV in the home. Others forbid mixed bathing, smoking, and drinking alcohol. Some even forbid coffee and tea. Others insist that worship must be on Saturday, the seventh day, and follow the dietary laws of the Old Testament (no pork ribs or visits to Red Lobster). When these matters become the basis on which Christians are judged, grace goes out the window. Sadly, acceptance in some churches is based on how well one can keep the rules. I spoke with a Catholic woman whose parish had recently installed a new priest. I asked her how she liked him. She said, "Oh, he's great. He won't let us get away with a thing." Many think it's easier to have a given set of rules to follow than to live their lives under the guidance of the Holy Spirit.

Substitutions for Scripture

Paul warned the people not to give *"heed to Jewish myths or to commands of men who reject the truth"* (Titus 1:14). There are certain clerics on the speaking circuit today who deny biblical truth and teach, as Gospel, *midrashim*, which is a collection of ancient Jewish commentaries on religious matters. They claim them to be a better source of truth than the scriptures themselves. A *midrash* is but a commentary or an interpretation of a biblical text. It may be interesting, but it does not have the authority of scripture.

Loading on the Burdens

In the first century, "those of the circumcision party" did not only vex Titus on the island of Crete, but troubled the Galatian church. In Paul's letter to them over an argument between grace and law, between believing and rule-keeping, he wrote, *"How can you compel the Gentiles to live like Jews?"* (Galatians 2:14). In J.B. Phillips' delightfully fresh translation of the New Testament, Paul says to the Galatians,

> *O you dear idiots of Galatia, who saw Jesus Christ the cruci-fied so plainly, who has been casting a spell over you? I will ask you one simple question: did you receive the Spirit of God by trying to keep the Law or by believing the message of the Gospel? Surely you can't be so idiotic as to think that a man begins his spiritual life in the Spirit and then completes it by reverting to outward observances?* (Galatians 3:1-3 Phillips).

These saints, though beloved, were abandoning the supernatural dimension of the faith. They had given up trusting the gracious influence of the Holy Spirit to change them, arguing that the way to become better Christians was to obey Jewish laws. Paul was always battling with those who tried to reduce Christ's work on the cross, declaring it incomplete until something was added. This was both to take away and to add on: take away grace and add on law; take away the power of the Holy Spirit and add on rule keeping.

65

Losing Our Assurance

Along the pilgrim way, some Christians become assailed by doubts about the quality of their faith. They feel that they have "backslidden." They begin to think that something more religious is required for them to be sure of their salvation. The troubled soul might say, "Maybe it will help me get back on track if I get busier in the Lord's work," and she turns to legalism. "Oughts" and "shoulds" become the new Gospel, which is no Gospel at all, for Gospel is Good News. It is a poor Gospel that cannot give a Christian assurance that Christ has done all that is needed for salvation. When Jesus, dying on the cross, cried, "It is finished," He was declaring that His work in providing salvation was now complete. From time to time we need to repent of the sin of trying to become more religious so God will love us more.

Other Christians know they are avoiding a central issue of obedience and try to cover their refusal to obey with churchy activity. Jesus has provided our salvation, but He calls each of us to obey as He did, even if that means giving up what we most want.

Just As I Am

Another problem that must be faced and eliminated is also an old one. Some say that certain conditions must be met before one can become a Christian: "You must get tidied up first and make some vows about future conduct." I have heard unbelievers say that they are not yet good enough to become Christians; that they will have to stop doing this and start doing that to be ready. Professor James Denney, over a hundred years ago, wrote

> "To try to take some preliminary security for the sinner's future morality before you make the gospel available to him is not only to strike at the root of assurance, it is to

pay a very poor tribute to the power of the gospel" (*The Death of Christ*, p. 161).

The old hymn, "Just as I am without one plea, but that Thy blood was shed for me" is always relevant. As Paul marvels, "He loved us even while we were still lost in our sinning" (Ephesians 2:5 author's paraphrase). We come to Jesus as we are, allow His blood to do its cleansing work in us, and then over the years and, in cooperation with Him, we grow to become more like Him.

The Awkward Receiver

We have heard that "It is more blessed to give than to receive" but for most of us "It is more difficult to receive than to give." It's a subtle thing but giving can make us feel superior and being on the receiving end makes us feel inferior. When we were building the Bezek Retreat Centre, we went through some hard times. One wintry day—while we still lived in the basement foundation—there was a knock on our door and a lady called out, "Where do you want us to put these?"

My wife called up, "What are they?"

The lady answered, "They are the white gifts from the church."

My wife received them, but she felt awkward. She said to me later, "When we were kids, we would bring our carefully wrapped white gifts to the church on Christmas White Gift Sunday. They were for the poor. And now we are the poor." It's not easy to be poor and be a good receiver.

Of course, the impoverished person's position is not helped when some people can't help feeling a bit superior when they give. Ready to leave the restaurant, I was waiting at the cashier to pay my bill when a beggar came in off the street. He put his arm on a well-dressed man who was also about to leave. The man pulled out some money, handed it to the cashier, and in a loud voice said, "Here! Give this bum a meal." Then he left with a smug look on his face. It was embarrassing to all of us who were within earshot, and it certainly was for the poor guy who was looking for a handout, not a put-down. Christ does not give the gift of salvation to humiliate us; He gives freely as to children, and we are to be simply grateful.

Earn Salvation or Deserve It?

If we receive a gift, we may feel embarrassed and not know how to react. We somehow feel uncomfortable unless we can give a gift of equal value in return. We don't like being in anyone's debt. When it comes to God, many of us, in our pride, feel that accepting His salvation without somehow earning it is not right. We distrust God's grace. We would rather think that by being good and doing good we can earn God's favour. God doesn't give wages, He gives gifts. When we are broken of pride and accept God's love and forgiveness, then we are set free to love Him and gratefully serve Him. But we can never match His generosity. The old gospel song says it well, "I had a debt I could not pay, He paid a debt He did not owe."

Good Works Misunderstood

Good works are expected from the Christian; but doing good works does not make God love us more. He cannot love us more than He already does, and nothing we can do will ever cause Him to love us less. When we truly trust God's finished work on the cross that gained us our salvation, the good works that we may now do are simply our response of gratitude for what God has done for us. Paul writes, *"By grace you have been saved through faith; and this is not your own doing, it is the gift of God—not because of works, lest any man should boast"* (Ephesians 2:8-9). First comes grace, then come the good works.

Working with God

St. Paul gave us the verse that says, *"Work out your own salvation with fear and trembling; for God is at work in you, both to will and to work for his good pleasure"* (Philippians 2:12-13). To each of us, God reveals His will, and as we agree to follow it, He works with us to fulfill it. The result is His good pleasure. Those who realize how much they have been forgiven gratefully forgive and serve others. We must not miss that part of the Gospel that asks obedience to Christ.

St. Augustine has often been quoted as saying, "Love God and do as you please." This saying contains the truth, but it doesn't give us a license for lawlessness. Augustine means that if we really love God we *will* do what pleases Him. Christians are given the privilege of seeing what God sees and, with the energy of the Holy Spirit, following His agenda. Jesus did say, *"If you love me, you will keep my commandments"* (John 14:15). He is speaking of His commandments, not those invented by people.

Messing Up the Response

He doesn't ask us to serve on every committee and take on every Christian task. To be ground down and beaten up by "doing the Lord's work" when somebody is bullying us or guilt is driving us means that we are not hearing Him well; that we are doing things not on God's agenda for us. That's not right. We need to receive His marching orders on our knees. One young evangelist told me, "I'm just so much in demand that I just can't take all the meetings that the Lord is sending me." I suspect that there was some misdirection of mail here. Christians need to learn how to subtract as well as add. To maintain Christian service over the long haul needs a balance of work and replenishing. But this is not a call to leisure, comfort, and self-indulgence—the so-called "good life" so many Christians have appropriated as a "right" by the standards of comfortable North Americans and Europeans.

Jesus calls us to lay down our lives, to take up our cross and follow Him. He calls us out into the deep waters of the needs of a world desperate for His answers—a world no further away than our community and answers that can only be found by walking with Him day by day and moment by moment, according to "every word that proceeds from the mouth of the Father." The road He calls us to travel entails sacrifice, perhaps even martyrdom. But if that calling is not God's but our own prideful vision of what we think might be a great idea, the sacrifice and the martyrdom will be useless in the Kingdom He is building. *"Though I give my body to be burned, but have not love, it profits me nothing,"* as Paul says (1 Corinthians 13:3 NKJV). God doesn't ask us to do more than we are able with Him. But we might do well to notice what some physically disabled or mentally challenged people accomplish; they awaken the rest of us about our God-given potential.

God didn't create us to be a company of driven religious slaves, but to be co-workers with the Holy Spirit in specific tasks He wants accomplished. Many Christians fail in worthy tasks because they tackle them in their own strength, not knowing how to pray on through the obstacles that Satan will throw into the path of good works. We must learn how to turn to Him not only for marching orders, but as our Guide every step of the way. If you have not yet approached a project prayerfully, knowing surely in your spirit what God wants to accomplish and learning as you walk together how you are to go about it, now is a good time to start.

God made us family. Families share family duties and also bless their neighbours. About 70 percent of the Canadian family considers themselves Christians; fewer than 20 percent attend church. They are believers, part of the Body of Christ; but we who consider ourselves leaders in the church or followers in the church are content to let most of our fellow Christians walk alone. That may be one place to start strengthening our organization to meet the challenges of a needy world.

The Twenty-first Century

Every generation faces new attempts to add on or take away from the Gospel. This generation certainly has its share. We face New Age teachings that declare men and women can be as gods and therefore can abandon God's ways and rewrite their own rules for living. For guidance, instead of searching the scriptures and praying, they listen to "the god within" or their "spirit guide." Among some Christians, blatant immorality is practiced, which is deliberately ignored by the church. Sometimes we find it among church leaders as well. Today we see a major erosion of the super-natural dimension of the Gospel, but an increase of occult interests, such as among those who reject the leading of the Holy Spirit to look at what astrologists say to do or not do on a given day. Many would take away the centrality of Jesus Christ to the faith in order to schmooze with other religions.

Help, Lord!

We may be tempted to cry out to the Lord to come and lift us out of all of this, but I have the feeling that we have more work to do and we had better be at it. God has promised to give us the strength and the power to be victorious. But let's not carry any more unnecessary baggage for the task. And let's not reject any grace that is available to help us with the task. Leaders, help your people to lighten the load that they might use their newly released energy for the day's tasks.

8

Losing the Ability to Lead: The Unstable Heart

Losing the Ability to Lead

When it comes down to the individual, whether a leader or a foot soldier, a divided heart will cause endless anxiety. As Jesus said, *"Every kingdom divided against itself will be ruined, and every city or house divided against itself will not stand"* (Matthew 12:25 NIV). The divided heart will stifle one's ability to hear God and to lead or to follow well. The Living Bible quotes Solomon as he wrote, *"The unfaithful are destroyed by their duplicity"* (Proverbs 11:3). One cannot be loyal to two conflicting calls and be at peace. Furthermore, inner harmony is conducive to physical and mental health.

Israel's King Saul was a man in conflict; the Bible describes the anxiety, the sleeplessness, and the suspicions of this man who had difficulty consistently obeying God. On any given day, he might be a faithful sovereign; on another day, he would do something perverse such as consulting a witch or throwing a spear at his servant David. He suffered for his sins, and eventually he did lose his throne and his divine mandate to lead. The prophet Samuel told him,

> *You acted foolishly...You have not kept the command the LORD your God gave you; if you had, he would have established your kingdom over Israel for all time. But now your kingdom will not endure* (1 Samuel 13:14 NIV).

Saul lost his focus; he lost his peace, and he lost his kingdom. If we are unfaithful, our well of grace will dry up and we will lose any influence we had in sharing the faith.

The Church's Heart

When Paul directed Titus to make the necessary corrections in the churches on the island of Crete, he was giving him a tall order. He was asked to *"amend what was defective"* (Titus 1:5). Paul is saying the same to us. There is no doubt that we could use some amending in many of our churches today. There is much discouragement, division, and lethargy among the people. Many leaders are theologically confused and some are morally compromised as well. Some leaders in the Cretan churches had to be replaced while others had to be disciplined. Today, groups and churches led by incompetent people or by men and women with major moral deficiencies—or that are in the middle of a dispute over the centrality of Jesus Christ, at war over worship styles, or are cold to newcomers—do not look attractive to prospective members. Who wants to join a fellowship and then have to choose sides in fights over doctrines and lifestyles? A stable fellowship that is alive, biblically grounded, and at peace will look much more attractive than one in chaos.

Sectarian Strife

Paul was an old hand at fighting fires of division in the church. You can almost see him wiping the sweat of frustration off his brow as he writes to the church at Corinth,

> *I appeal to you, brothers, in the name of our Lord Jesus Christ, that all of you agree with one another so that there may be no divisions among you and that you may be perfectly united in mind and thought* (1 Corinthians 1:10 NIV).

He went on to say,

My brothers, some from Chloe's household have informed me that there are quarrels among you. What I mean is this: One of you says, "I follow Paul"; another, "I follow Apollo"; another, "I follow Cephas"; still another, "I follow Christ." Is Christ divided? Was Paul crucified for you? (1 Corinthians 1:11-13 NIV).

Paul had his hands full dealing with the factions in the Corinthian church, and he is saying to Titus, "You have to handle this business of divided loyalties in Crete, too."

From its earliest days, the church has produced factions. Now, we think that our major divisions and the denominations that arose out of old church fights have been sanctified by time and history. Catholics, Protestants, Orthodox, and Pentecostals all look to the past to justify who they are, how they are governed, what they practice, and what they believe. Today some divisions may not be over theology but how to worship. It's hard to find common ground between a church that worships with a noisy band of guitars, drums, and keyboards as they sing up-beat choruses and another church that believes only traditional ("old favourite") hymns, accompanied by a pipe organ and a gowned choir, are appropriate. Some have no ordained clergy; others have priests who swing incense pots. Some pastors preach in blue jeans while others wear a Geneva gown, clerical collar, hood, tabs, and stole. Some churches hand out a printed, eight-page order-of-service bulletin while others just wing it. Can we have grace to accept one another? We try.

Bad Health

Churches are torn, but what about the people who make up these churches? Paul tells us that Christians can become sick and even die because of their actions and attitudes (1 Corinthians 11:30). Modern medicine also knows that stress can damage the body's immune system. Only a fool thinks that an illicit affair carried on by a husband or wife does not affect every member of the family for ill. Even if the affair is secretive, it gnaws away at the peace of the home. The man who is cheating in his business is on edge every time his office phone rings, and if anyone looks sideways at him in a meeting, he thinks, "That man knows." If there is conflict in the heart, there comes a sickness where expressing the joy of the Lord has to be forced. William James wrote, "Religion in its broadest and most general terms possible...consists of the belief that there is an 'Unseen Order' and that our supreme good lies in adjusting ourselves thereto." Putting it another way, "Following God's ways brings inner peace."

A Divided Congregation

It's interesting to note that there are not only major differences between denominations but many differences can be found within one congregation. One church may include irritating social activists, haughty evangelicals, and boisterous charismatics. There are moral tut-tutters whose favourite word is "no." They stress external "holy" conduct while others opt for the freedom to smoke a cigar, drink a glass of wine, and go to horse races. There may be Word-oriented people who lean heavily on the scriptures but who are suspicious of any manifestation of the Spirit's presence. "Over-the-top" Spirit-oriented people may come perilously close to neglecting decency and order (1 Corinthians 14:40) in favour of seeking emotional experiences that the Spirit might bring. At budget time, people can get a little testy. "Should we buy the new organ or send the money to help the people of Darfur in the Sudan?" "Do we redecorate the Sunday-school rooms, or do we give that money to the local food bank?" "We need more money in the budget for the youth." "But what about us seniors, we have needs too." The questions go on and on. It's a wonder that any given congregation does not fly apart into six different splinters.

Many of the letters of the New Testament deal with difficulties in the churches over which Paul had apostolic authority. Also, the first three chapters of the Revelation of John show us Jesus confronting the seven churches in Asia Minor about their sins and failings. After giving each one an encouraging word of praise, He lists its faults of wrongdoing and wrong believing. These problems were damaging to their health and prevented them from sharing love and truth to those around them. Pride, lethargy, condoning immoral conduct, allowing false prophets to speak in the assembly, and the cooling of their love for Him are noted with sadness. Jesus threatened to put their lights out if they did not shape up. The truth today is that many churches have long since become darkened by unbelief and lack of love.

Torn to Pieces

Perhaps the most extreme example of a divided heart is found in Mark's story of the Gadarene demoniac. In this gospel, Jesus has just stilled the storm on the sea and then lands, with His disciples, on the shores of Gadara. He instantly is confronted by a crazy man coming out of the tombs who is possessed by an unclean spirit. He is a tormented, desperate man who cuts himself on the rocks in the caves. He breaks the chains put on him by those who seek to restrain him. He frightens everyone who comes near and yet, on seeing Jesus, he immediately begins to worship Him. When Jesus asks the demon its name, he is told, "Legion, for we are many." Jesus casts out the demons, and they go into a herd of pigs, which run headlong down a hill into the sea (Mark 5:1-13). Whatever the original cause of the man's condition, he was a lonely, "torn-to-pieces" man, pulled this way and that by evil forces within. Jesus faced those forces, silenced them, and cast them out. The Gadarene's war was over. His personality became integrated, and he was made whole. Here was a new man, sitting quietly, fully clothed, and in his right mind.

Something of the man from Gadara may be in each of us at times in our life. We, too, have forces within that pull us this way and that; forces for good, forces for ill. They are not necessarily demonic forces, but in the extreme, the results are similar. It takes the love, the forgiveness, the Word, and the healing of Jesus to begin to put us together. When we speak of a person as being "really together," we mean that she is heading in one basic direction and not six. We mean that he is not overly distracted by conflicting demands and refuses to give in to those things that would pull him off course. Modern life has so many demands. There are claims of family, work, church, exercise, charity, golf, service club, work around the house and the garden. The children need help with their homework and counselling about drugs, sex, and alcohol, and rides to soccer practices. The list goes on. Some claims are noisily persistent while legitimate ones such as teaching disciplines of prayer and Bible study are barely heard. Many things compete for our energy, time, and money. Some important ones get the short end of our time and energy.

We Need Help

In order to lead well, we need other seasoned believers to mentor us and call us to account. We need help in exorcizing what is destructive. There is no room for an illicit affair, secret drinking, gambling, or drug use. There is no place for pornography or wasting our energy planning revenge over a real or imagined hurt. Fantasizing over another person silently wounds the relationship with one's spouse. *"Cleanse your hands, ye sinners; and purify your hearts, ye double-minded,"* says James 4:8 (KJV). Let us be open to

Jesus, transparent to our spouse, available to our children, and dependable and consistent in our relationships at work, in the church, and about the neighbourhood. We need to allow Jesus to be the Lord in our lives, and we need godly mentors to help us to structure our lives in a way that works.

The Stable Heart

James writes, *"A double minded man is unstable in all his ways"* (James 1:8 KJV). Jesus declared that, *"And if a house is divided against itself, that house will not be able to stand"* (Mark 3:25). The cure for a divided mind is to prayerfully try to find out God's agenda and work to that. The cure for a divided church will follow from people who have dealt with their inner conflicts. Try to exclude distractions, whether they are noisy or quiet. Allow the Holy Spirit to prune from your tree of life the suckers that bear no fruit. Jesus said, *"My Father is the gardener...while every branch that does bear fruit he prunes so that it will be even more fruitful"* (John 15:1-2 NIV). Life can be simplified, sweetened, and empowered by letting God define your agenda of activities and your relationships.

9

Leaders and Followers: Together for a Purpose

Why Do We Get Together?

When I was the pastor of Alderwood United Church in the 1960s, many of the churches in our West Toronto area were struggling. A firm of sociologists was hired to find out why. As the pastor, I was asked to gather my twelve most influential church people to meet with one of their people. The sociologist, a man in his early thirties, came to our gathered dozen, introduced himself, and, without preamble, asked, "What is this church for?" There was a short pause and then we began to tell him of our worship and our desire to bring people to Christ. We spoke of our programs for youth, our teaching seminars to help one another towards Christian maturity and to fulfill our callings as Christians. Our twelve had a lot to say.

When we had said our piece, our visitor told us that of the half-dozen churches he had visited thus far, we were the only one that didn't sputter at his question. He said, "When I asked them the same question I asked you, I got responses like 'Well, like, uh everybody knows what the church is for. You know, I mean, ah, uh, well, somebody tell him.' It's strange," he said. "These were the people who were responsible for leading their church, but most of them had difficulty articulating what their church was there for." I was saddened to hear that, but I was quietly pleased with the ability of our twelve to give reasons for our being a church. Doesn't it make sense to know why we are in business? Why we do get together?

The Goal

A good leader must know where God wants the people to go and be able to convince others to come along. As individuals, every believer's goal is to become a mature Christian. In St. Paul's letter to the Ephesians, we read that the resurrected and ascended Christ gave five ministry gifts to the church: apostles, prophets, evangelists, pastors, and teachers. Without going into their specific job descriptions, they had one main purpose, which was *"to equip the saints for the work of ministry, for building up the body of Christ"* (Ephesians 4:12). The leader's plan and prayer is that he or she become equipped, along with his or her co-workers, for the work of the ministry. The goal of the ministry is to build up the Body of Christ—the Church. We reach out to people, introducing them to Jesus Christ. Then, as they are willing, we lead them towards maturity with teaching, coaching, and by example. With new insight and with moral integrity, we help each other learn to live the Christian life in our homes and in the working world.

The First Requirement

A young man I know trained to be a pastor. He was ordained and sent to his first church. He had been there for about a year when he invited me to come and preach to his people. While chatting before the service I asked him how things were going.

He said, "Not very well. They won't believe what I tell them, and they won't do what I ask them."

I thought a minute before asking, "Do you love your people?"

He became defensive and said, "Why should I love them if they won't follow my lead?"

My response was, "Why should they follow your lead if they don't think you love them? What kind of a shepherd is that?" The first requirement of a leader is to love his people as they are. Only then will they trust him enough to start following. It's not how far and how fast a leader can travel that counts; it's how well he brings others along with him. You could call this the pace of love. Someone has said, "If a man thinks he is a leader and heads out at a great rate to reach his goal and then finds that no one is following, he is not leading, he is just taking a walk."

A Christian minister had served the church well. He died in old age and his funeral was a large one. I was not present, but I read his published obituary. The key sentence for me in the obituary was, "During his ministry, many entered the Kingdom because of his gracious invitation." You can't do better than that. He loved the people he was called to serve. They listened to him, and he graciously invited them, as they were ready, to enter into a loving relationship with Jesus. He was a caring leader. In contrast, we read in the Bible about King Jehoram of Judah. He was a faithless and uncaring leader, and when he died it was written of him, *"He passed away, to no one's regret"* (2 Chronicles 21:20 NIV).

Offering a Lesser God

Some of us got into the church through a side door. I was confirmed as a twelve-year-old following some instruction about the organization of the church, but the Gospel was not explained. I lived for years with a weak definition of the Christian faith. After a short career in civil engineering, I began studying for the ministry. One summer, when I was a student, my job was to canvass homes in some of Toronto's new subdivisions to find people willing to become members of the church planned for their area. Knocking on doors, I said that a church would be a good thing for their community and invited them to be a part of it. When I asked them if they would like to "join the church," a typical response was, "I guess so." Instead of sharing with them the Gospel of the Lord Jesus Christ and inviting them to become part of His Church, I was recruiting people to join a religious organization that might provide some cultural morality in their new community. Because at that time I didn't know any better, I failed to give them a biblical view of the church. Although some understood the gospel and believed it, we mainly enlisted people who had some church background and wanted a church so their kids might get some moral teaching plus a bit of religion. For many, their creed was "I guess so"—not exactly a powerful statement of faith.

Cause, Effect, and Remedy

Lost Joy

Even a church that knows the Gospel may go through dry times. At first it is alive and exciting, but then things flatten out. The sparkle and the joy are gone, and people are coming just out of habit. There could be hidden problems. I know a little church in Ontario's near north that the Lord visited with revival. People were being converted and healed. Members were excited to do personal evangelism, and folks came long distances to find the life that was being poured out there. The revival continued for a time, but then things began to cool off. Conversions were rare, and personal evangelism petered out. The joy slowly evaporated. People began to wander off. Musical groups were brought in to help liven things up. Evangelists were invited to come and stir up the people, but the response was minimal. Why?

The Remedy

The four elders of this little church gathered to fast and pray about the situation. They suggested possible ways to restore life in the church. Nothing they suggested seemed to be the answer to their spiritual drought. They met weekly for some months. One evening, an elder confessed his unhappiness at conditions in the church and then blurted out that perhaps he was part of the problem. He told of hiring a local carpenter to build a porch for his house. In a dispute over the cost, the matter was never settled. He said he would pay the carpenter what he had asked. That confession encouraged another elder to admit that he had fired an employee for stealing. He said that later he found that the money had just been misplaced. Pride kept him from going to the man, asking forgiveness, and offering him his job back. He would make it right. Other sins were confessed that night and repentance expressed.

It was not long before a refreshing spirit began to touch the church. The people were eager to be there. They brought unbelieving neighbours who became converted. The Spirit was again free to move among them. St. Peter preached, *"Repent, then, and turn to God, so that your sins may be wiped out, that times of refreshing may come from the Lord"* (Acts 3:19 NIV). Repentance is a repeatable event.

Clarifying Decision Making and Responsibility

When one is leading a group, whether in business, church, sports, family, or farm, it contributes greatly to the peace and success of the venture when individuals know what is expected of them. During the eighteen years I was responsible for leading a little company of people in the building and operating of Bezek, a retreat and healing centre, there were times when I was so occupied with my own work that I failed to make my expectations known to the others. They often had to guess what I wanted of them. Since all were volunteers and getting no salary, I felt awkward about being the boss. It was a mixed bunch that the Lord had brought together. Some asked for more direction while others preferred to be left alone to figure out for themselves what to do. There were some chaotic times. We worked best when I had the confidence to share my visions and dreams with them and took the courage to spell out their tasks to help make them happen. The staff didn't need a lot of rules to follow, although some rules were necessary; they needed some good ongoing direction concerning their responsibilities and an understanding of what we were called to do and where we were to go.

Instructing with Confidence

Paul told Titus, *"Encourage and rebuke with all authority. Do not let anyone despise you"* (Titus 2:15 NIV). Godly power is exercised not by bullying, but by giving clear direction (within one's sphere of authority) with a grace that convinces people to respond without feeling put upon. Where correction is needed, it should be given without couching it in a joke or in some other off-handed way, hoping they'll get the message. Good leaders create an atmosphere where others are secure enough to understand that "correction is not rejection." Flaunted authority produces fear and rebellion. Authority, graciously exercised, brings peace and does not produce a "Yes, but" concerning every request.

Paul told Titus that he should be able to give instruction (Titus 2:6). He was to confidently teach the content of the Gospel as well as to spell out its application. The leader articulates the goal and outlines the tasks needed to reach it, then, with enthusiasm, leads the troops in getting on with it. *Laissez-faire* leadership, which simply leaves people to find their own way, is not leadership at all. Dictatorship is worse. Jesus said, *"I am among you as one who serves"* (Luke 22:27). A good leader serves the people by giving them clear direction, enabling them to help fulfill the claims of the Kingdom and to become mature in doing so. A wise leader also will be willing to train a successor. It's important to delegate to others some of the responsibilities of leadership to prepare them for the day when they will be called to lead, even as God called Moses to prepare Joshua for leadership that lay ahead (Numbers 27:18).

Dare To Have a Purpose Firm

One of the songs I learned as a boy in Sunday school was, "Dare To Be a Daniel." It is based on the Old Testament story of the young Hebrew man taken into captivity, who knew who he was and what he believed. He suffered for his principles, but he didn't back down even before lions. The one line I remember so well from the song was, "Dare to have a purpose firm and dare to make it known." I believe that being part of a group can enable a person not to hide from the world, but to be strengthened and emboldened to engage the world. We are commissioned to share with others the validity of Christ's way and show an inevitably faulty but nevertheless real example of one who is trying to be His disciple; one who has a good idea of why she or he is here.

Does your group have an identifiable purpose? Does your business, group, or church have a clear vision and can you make it known? A wise project of organizations is to create a "Mission Statement." Every group should have, both on paper and also written in their hearts, an understandable answer to a similar question the young sociologist asked of our congregational leadership, "What's this church for?" He would ask, "What's your group for?" Can you say it? Can you put it in writing? Is it written on your heart? Is it happening? Are you praying?

10

What Motivates People

Goals

To be motivated, we need identifiable goals. In the Christian walk, people will study the Word and wrestle in their prayers for the reward of knowing God better and, in a lesser way, to keep up with others in their study group. We are motivated by rewards of one kind or another. Paul speaks of the long-range reward for the struggle—that of coming to unity in faith and mature manhood (Ephesians 4:13). But most of us seem to need short-range and more quickly reached goals to keep us interested. We want to see tangible results and see them soon. When we reach one goal, we need another. If the church embarks on a building program, the finished building is the goal. The members will dig, hammer, canvass for money, and give. They will meet on committees late into the night. The goal is the completed building. Then what?

Seeing Results

As a young minister, I was given the task of gathering people who might be interested in forming a Protestant church in the mostly French-speaking and Roman Catholic town of Chelmsford, a few miles northwest of Sudbury. My wife, Dorla, and I knocked on many doors and convinced a handful of souls to gather for worship. We met in Stewart's living room, and I played my accordion for the hymns. Later we met in the Salle des Copains dance club hall. We moved into Tommy Deminion's welding shop and later into the public school. Then we hired an architect to design us a simple building that would hold about sixty people. Part of what kept us going was the prospect of someday having a church building of our own.

We got a piece of land, begged and borrowed some money for materials, and then started to build. Townspeople who had little interest in the Christian faith became enthusiastic about something happening in their little town, even a new church building. Men from any denomination, or none, came and laid blocks, set windows, raised trusses, did plumbing, and put up drywall. We did it all with volunteer labour. My father, who was then well on in years, came to visit, and I found him up on the roof nailing shingles. We got a bell from a retired steam locomotive, and somebody brought us two poles for the hydro hook up. I was told not to ask where he got them. Everybody was keen, and in a matter of eight months, we finished the building.

Celebration Day

On the afternoon of the day of dedication, along with a number of church dignitaries, over 100 people crowded into the little church with many more standing outside. We had a youth choir sing and heard speeches from various citizens. With great fanfare, St. Stephen's United Church was dedicated. It was an exciting afternoon. Following the service, we had a celebration dinner in the Legion Hall, 150 strong. We had a great party with more speeches. (Out of respect for the clergy present, they didn't open the bar.)

What Next?

The following Sunday, I was really excited to get to our new church for the service. I was sure we would be crowded out. The hour of worship arrived, and to my disappointment, there were the usual eighteen or twenty who had been with us from the beginning. I was confused. People seemed so pleased to be part of the construction project. To see it finished was their goal. I had been unable to convince them that there was more to it than just seeing the building completed and dedicated. I guess most people (me included) want speedy gratification or at least some goal or reward that is visible and not too far off. When we reach it, we need something new to look forward to.

Longer-term Goals

Those who run youth groups in the church are always scratching to find something that will keep the interest of the kids. Adults, actually, seem to require the same. But what about long-term spiritual goals? What will motivate us to see beyond the immediate and concrete? St. Paul writes, *"Forgetting what lies behind and straining forward to what lies ahead, I press on toward the goal for the prize of the upward call of God in Christ"* (Philippians 3:14). We need to be constantly growing, understanding, and serving. Most of us are still at the stage where St. Paul writes, *"But I, brethren, could not address you as spiritual men, but as men of the flesh, as babes in Christ. I fed you with milk, not solid food; for you were not ready for it; and even yet you are not ready"* (1 Corinthians 3:1-2).

Milestones

Is life just a sequence of events? There are milestones along the road of life. As a small boy, getting out of short pants and wearing long trousers was a milestone. Then, it was off to high school, university, career, marriage, raising children, then their marriages; baby-sitting their children, getting old, retiring, and walking the downward trail with our "wounds of age," including arthritis, prostate problems, high blood pressure, fading memory, and then death. That's the human side. Life may be interesting, but that end sounds bleak. It *is* bleak without a hope for something beautiful awaiting us at the end.

But there can be parallel milestones along the way—spiritual ones. As youths, most of us were exposed to Christian things: stories, ideas, images, places, celebrations. As teens we experienced times of indifference to spiritual matters. Then we looked for meaning to our existence and considered faith. Perhaps we fell in with some Christians and joined up with them. Then came conversion and, in our new-found enthusiasm, we led others to faith. We grew in grace and insight. Then came a period of doubting and disillusionment, with backsliding and a season of spiritual drought. Then we were shaken by a crisis. Faith was renewed. We started getting serious about maturing. Finding God's purpose for our lives motivated us to get into the scriptures again. Somewhere along the way we were called to leadership. All the while, there was the oft-times hesitant response to the upward call of Christ to follow Him and to become like Him. As we grew older, we faced death, not as the end, but as the start of a new journey with the Father and Son we have come to trust. But while we live we must ask, "How do we make the best use of our time? If we are called to lead, how can we be good leaders?"

How Not To Lead

At one time in my pastoral ministry, I had an organist/choirmaster who lacked the confidence and/or the willingness to lead. At choir practice, he would ask his choir members, "Now, I'm not sure of this part, how do you think it should go?" Or, "What anthem do you think we should sing this Sunday? This one? Perhaps something else." He drove his choristers crazy with his dithering indecision, his refusal to lead when that was what was required of him. A choir leader trying to operate democratically is a disaster. Many were glad when he decided to move on. My son Dan, who is an orchestra conductor, does not operate democratically with his musicians. His job description requires him to choose and learn the music. He must rehearse his musicians, motivating them with his own enthusiasm to learn their parts and enjoy their rehearsals. Because he is disciplined, he has the confidence to discipline them. Then, with confidence and skill, he conducts them in concert to offer his audience great music.

Differing Styles

In my engineering days on construction projects, I saw all kinds of leadership and lack of it. Some of it was bullying, some encouraging, some passive. I heard one superintendent ask his foreman how many men he had fired in the last week. "None," he said.

"Don't tell me that you have a perfect crew; get rid of your two most incompetent men, and do it today."

Bosses have the power of the purse—to hire and fire, promote and demote. Union leaders have great influence over a decision whether to strike or not. However, in the Christian life, we as leaders have very little power. What we *can* have is influence. If we try to control people, they will respond with a sullen attitude or say, "I don't need this," and walk away. If, as leaders, we forget about trying to exert power over people and use godly influence instead, we will inspire and encourage them to serve and grow. We need a vision and for the people to catch it. They will respond to that kind of leadership, and good things can happen. We need to offer the right balance of authority and permission. Too little rule invites anarchy; too much rule is tyranny.

No Vision

In the Wisdom of Solomon, there is a proverb that can be translated from the Hebrew in a number of ways. From various versions of the Bible, here are a few different translations of Proverbs 29:18: *"Where there is no vision, the people perish"* (KJV) and *"Where there is ignorance of God the people run wild."* But I like the translation that says, *"Where there is no one in charge the people just stand around."* There are religious groups that die while others run wild. But saddest of all is the group whose people just stand around going nowhere because there is no leadership with vision. Where there is no direction or motivation, there is no fruitful life.

Jesus Is the Way, the Truth, and the Life

We are people of the Spirit. St. Paul writes, "If the Spirit is the source of your life, let the Spirit direct the course of your life" (Galatians 5:25 author's paraphrase). We are not earth-bound creatures. We cannot just look to the next barbecue to raise funds for the painting of the church or the upcoming golf tournament to keep the guys interested in being part of the fellowship. Jesus said to Peter and John, "Follow Me." He did not control men; He did not bully them, nor did He promise them pretty trinkets as rewards. He promised them a life with meaning. He also allowed them to say, "No." Our journey calls for hearing and following Jesus, who goes before us, leading us on the upward trail of serving, loving, and sharing the good news of His salvation. He gives us the gift of human leaders who interpret His agenda and lead us in His ways. Maturity is our earthly goal, heaven our final goal. Our business is to bring as many with us as we can; both to maturity and to heaven. That's the task for leaders; it's also the joy of every follower of the Lord Jesus.

11

Priorities of the Fellowship

Getting Together

Christians are asked to get together. The Hebrew letter tells us, *"Let us consider how to stir up one another to love and good works, not neglecting to meet together, as is the habit of some, but encouraging one another"* (Hebrews 10:25). For some, getting together isn't a high priority and most have no concept of what "stirring one another up to love and good works" means. Some Christians attend worship out of family tradition. As Sir George McLeod of Iona put it, "They come to worship at the tomb of their ancestors." Others attend when it's convenient.

One Sunday I was guest preacher in a fairly affluent church. A few minutes after the service ended, a car pulled up to the front door. Two men in golfing clothes got out, came into the church, and took the offering away. No doubt, after finishing their eighteen holes, they dutifully counted and banked it. That spring Sunday, golf trumped worship. In winter, it may have been curling that provided the draw. But if the truth were to be known, some avoid attending worship because there is nothing there for them and they see no way of making a contribution because the Old Guard is firmly in place and all the bases are covered. Someone has said that in too many churches on a

Sunday morning "The hungry sheep look up and they are not fed."

Getting Each Other Going

The scripture says that we are to *"stir up one another to love and good works."* We are to encourage one another. If these are the priorities of the church, why do we sit in rows looking at the back of the head of the one in front of us, perhaps speaking to one another after the service but only in superficialities? We're missing something. A few dozen may stay for the coffee and chatter, but most only talk to those they know and conversation rarely reaches the person hiding inside the individual. I heard this greeting one morning as I entered church, "Good morning, Louise, how are you?"

She replied, "Do you really want to know?"

Embarrassed, he answered, "No." Then, turning away, it was a quick "Good morning, Charlie...." I know there was no time to go into Louise's concerns right then, but when would he find out how she really was and be able to help? How can we get together to share our lives in a meaningful way? How can we crack the veneer of self-sufficiency and find the energy to get to know one another?

Smaller Is Better

People need to find ways they can meet on a regular basis and begin to relate to one another at an increasingly deeper level. Call them small groups, house fellowships, Bible study groups, men's groups, kin groups, women's groups, youth groups, or prayer groups. For meaningful interaction, groups should not be too large, perhaps a dozen or fifteen people. The Acts of the Apostles says that the Christians were *"day by day, attending the temple together and breaking bread in their homes"* (Acts 2:46). Previously the record reads, *"They devoted themselves to the apostles' teaching...the breaking of bread and the prayers"* (Acts 2:42). This tells us that the Christians gathered in large numbers to attend temple worship and they also met in smaller groups for teaching, discussion, prayer, and a common meal. We need to be part of the whole congregation on Sunday and then, perhaps, mid-week in smaller groups. We need to worship together and also have the more intimate setting where we can know and serve one another better. There could also be groups that have no connection to a particular church but are gathered on some other basis, such as men who work in the same office or factory meeting over lunch.

Leading in the Small Group

Perhaps, like Titus, you have been assigned to lead under your pastor's authority. What are the priorities of the small group? We have to know who we are, what we are about. As the old Scottish folk song says, "I know where I'm goin' and I know who's goin' wi' me." We need to be willing to help one another along the way. To do that, we must learn to spot a person's pain or spiritual hunger.

Does a man answer "I'm fine" to a brother's "How are you?" because he is not sure that the brother really cares? The wrong question is asked and a shallow answer is given (which is sometimes a lie). A little specific probing might produce a quiet, "Have you got a couple of minutes?" Then real communication takes place. The Jewish greeting to another is sometimes, *"Maschlemha."* It means more than "How are you?" It means "Are you complete?" We can help one another by taking the time to find out what's missing. But honest sharing doesn't happen unless there's a basis for trust.

Confidentiality

A priority of fellowship is confidentiality. Too often one hears something like this: "Now I'm just sharing this so that you will be able to pray, but did you know that...?" Some of us are really gossiping, pretending that we only share this information so that people can pray about it. It could be both. If in doubt, don't say it. If it's not your business, don't ask about it. Don't even be curious. Honour a word given in confidence. Sharing can only be frank and healing take place when the person sharing knows that the members of the small group can be counted on not to gossip.

If you doubt that the members of the group can do this, your first priority as a leader will be teaching the necessity for confidentiality and leading people to pray for sensitivity and love towards their group members.

Levels of Sharing

Sometimes in a mixed fellowship that grows close, a relationship may spring up that is too intimate. When men and women are together in spiritual and physical proximity and sexual hunger surfaces, there can be one hug too long, one wrongly motivated expression of "love," one confidence that ought not to have been shared, and a line is crossed. A vulnerable man listening to a vulnerable woman telling about her marriage difficulties can change a relationship that is "in Christ" to one that is in the flesh. Soul-mating is not scriptural. The Holy Spirit does free us from our oppressions, and if our false inhibitions are not sorted from proper self-control under His guidance, disaster can follow. The late E. Stanley Jones, that great Methodist missionary to India, said, "Sharing is helpful, but for some things, God has a private office." Keeping the right balance of frankness and considerate respect is essential when the social barriers between the sexes are as thin as they are today. A wise leader will establish and model ground rules that protect privacy and curb inappropriate intimacy.

Where Healing Can Take Place

The leader alone cannot take care of all the pastoral needs in a group but needs to see that those needs are addressed. The gifts of the Holy Spirit are to be found in all of those who participate in the Spirit's life. Gifts of discernment enable us to determine root causes of disturbances that erupt from troubled people. Gifts of healing available for those who are sick that may be administered by those who have faith to pray for healing. Gifts of wisdom and knowledge can enlighten the fellowship when there is uncertainty. In 1 Corinthians 12:8-10, St. Paul lists some of the gifts that are available to the Body of Christ, the Church. We need to learn how to access the healing available through the Holy Spirit without abandoning human wisdom and medical techniques. Prayers for healing of those suffering emotional pain can be offered as needs arise and there will be those who are comfortable in doing this.

Dare To Discipline

Much nonsense can go on in a person's life that interferes with the good of the family, the job, and the fellowship. One person may be spreading rumours by slandering another; a couple may be trying to introduce false doctrine; some may be sowing seeds of dissention and division. "Factious and quarrelsome," Paul calls such people (Titus 3:10). One may be a hurting soul who is simply expressing the confusion within from some earlier rejection.

Scripture tells us how to correct and discipline those who are out of line and upsetting the peace. We do it always in love, for the person's well-being, and for love of the members of the fellowship, who too often suffer under unchecked foolishness from the troubled and the troublemaker. Do not postpone dealing with discord or it will infect the whole group.

Correction Using the Word

Paul writes, *"All scripture is inspired by God and profitable for teaching, for reproof, for correction, and for training in righteousness"* (2 Timothy 3:16). Reproof and correction need to be applied, without being heavy handed, by going quietly to the person and asking him or her to change the ungodly behaviour. If the person will not hear you, then two or three others must go and reason with the person. Failing that, the person is to be brought before the group and corrected. If he or she will not receive it, let the person go. (See Matthew 18:15-17.) God's Wisdom says, *"My son, despise not the chastening of the LORD; neither be weary of his correction: For whom the LORD loveth he correcteth; even as a father the son in whom he delighteth"* (Proverbs 4:11-12 KJV).

Mentoring By Example, Teaching, and Correction

Some people, on receiving correction, will say, "Thanks. I needed to hear that." But most of us resent being disciplined, and most of us in leadership find it hard to administer correction. Security and peace are the marks of a group in which nonsense is confronted and error corrected in love.

Looking at the life of Jesus in Mark 3:13-14 (The Message), we find something of His style. *"He climbed a mountain and invited those he wanted with him. They climbed together."* He modelled life for them and had no hesitation in confronting ego, bad theology, or foolishness among His disciples. But mentoring is not—except in the case of Jesus—one guy sitting on a perch of perfection telling someone, "Do this or do that." Mentoring means teaching by word and example and also by sharing pain and flaws together. It means convincing another that walking in Christ's way is the greatest way to travel this planet.

Whadda Ya Say, Coach?

Before becoming a preacher, I was an engineer. For a few years, my job allowed me time to play and coach lacrosse. I coached boys in their middle and late teens. What I learned about leadership in coaching was of help to me in the pastorate: motivation is essential. "We can win this game!" and "We can meet this mortgage payment!" are not so different. In lacrosse practice, it was, "Cover your man, clean up your language, straighten your shot, run harder, keep your eyes open, and know who's got the ball." The same instructions can be seen in St. Paul's admonitions to Titus. Take a minute to make your own note of the parallels. I had to deal with fear because often our opponents were bigger and stronger. "But we're faster and smarter," I said. I had to slow down the over-zealous and stir up the unwilling. Correction and discipline were part of the drill.

Some leadership principles apply alike to sports, business, and the Christian life. Leading a group of any kind requires enthusiasm, patience, and caring. I don't remember praying for my lacrosse players (I wasn't a Christian yet) but I found out, years later, that praying for the people of my congregation was a vital part of caring for them.

About Sharing

The early church didn't seem to have much trouble sharing stuff with one another. The scripture says they *"had all things in common; and they sold their possessions and goods and distributed them to all, as any had need"* (Acts 2:44-45). That's scary, isn't it? I may not mind lending my lawnmower to a neighbour, but I would have to be mightily moved to again start living in a fellowship that shares a common purse. When my wife and family and I were part of the small group of seven or eight operating Bezek retreat and healing centre, we gave communal finances a try. One of our group was a school teacher. Her income was put into the purse as were the honorariums I received from speaking. The others had little or no income. Each of us had to justify any felt need to draw from the common purse. I found it was tough to have to ask for money for new underwear. This experiment survived for about two years. It was a useful learning time, but we eventually emptied the community purse and reverted to a more voluntary helping of one another financially.

Sharing Isn't Easy

When is it right to give real money, loan our car, or share our house with a family out of work? We had to try it to see. We were taken advantage of; there were freeloaders who had no thought of helping. We had to be careful to make sure our children were protected. Hospitality is both a gift and a learned part of lifestyle. We need to be *"wise as serpents and innocent as doves"* (Matthew 10:16). I just know that if all our money is the Lord's money, we might be strongly led to give some of it away to a needy brother. If our house is the Lord's, we might need to share it sometime and so "do good to one another for Christ's sake." Paul told Titus that a leader must be *"a lover of hospitality"* (Titus 1:8 KJV), and St. Peter wrote, *"Offer hospitality to one another"* (1 Peter 4:9 NIV). Can we let people into our lives in ways that inconvenience us? Fellowship can mean little or much.

Christianity Is Radical Living

The true Christian culture is a counter culture. It is opposed to the selfish ways of the world. It lives Christ's teaching in the Sermon on the Mount (Matthew 5, 6, and 7). If we really live the Christian life, our goals are different from those of the world, our possessions less important, and our faith relationships mutually beneficial in things small and large. A small group is a good place to begin to do as Paul asked, *"Examine yourselves to see whether you are in the faith"* (2 Corinthians 13:5 NIV). This kind of commitment is living as the scripture says, "Stirring up one another to love and good works" (Hebrews 10:24).

Above All: Jesus

Some people in your group may not have made a commitment to Jesus Christ. They may enjoy the fellowship and participate in its activities but not yet have invited Jesus into their lives. My experience is that many in the churches of today have neither been offered the joy of salvation nor been called to respond to an invitation to receive it. A good leader will want to know where his flock stands spiritually, and those who are still outside the Kingdom can be led into taking this most important step in their lives (John 3:3).

To Take This Step

The Bible teaches us that our sin has created a separation between us and God. He wants to bring us back to Himself. Jesus is that Way back. Sincerely praying a prayer such as this will open the door for a new life to begin:

"God, I confess that I am a sinner. I am sorry for my sins. I believe that You sent Jesus, Your Son, to die on the cross, shedding His blood to make me clean.

"Jesus, I believe You are risen from the dead and are here with me now, loving me. I ask You to come into my life, forgive me, and make me new.

"I commit my life to You and with Your help I will serve You all my life.

"Thank You. Amen."

12

Faithless Shepherds and Faithless Sheep

When Leaders Fall

On the back cover of this book, I name the four main traps into which leaders may fall: money, power, sex, and isolation from peers. If a gifted leader grows in the public eye and his ministry becomes successful, acclaim and adulation may make him think quite highly of himself. His ego is puffed. As he becomes a public figure, he might believe that his success is due to God, who will protect him from ever falling. He may be conscious of personal flaws, but because he continues to be successful, he feels that his success is a sign of God's approval and that God overlooks these flaws or He would have taken away his gifting. A scripture open to interpretation may be seized on, such as "God has said in His word that *'the gifts and the call of God are irrevocable'*"(Romans 11:29).

As his platform is enlarged, women become sexually attracted to him. Groupies congregate, and followers give him gifts. He begins to think himself invincible. He shuts himself off from the counsel of his peers and delights in the money that comes pouring in, which he begins to use for his own pleasure. As the foundation of integrity begins to crumble, so the edifice of ministry begins to tilt and one major indiscretion will cause him to fall. Thus does God bring him down. The crash is noted by Christian and unbeliever alike. The cause of Christ is damaged. The higher the profile, the greater the fall.

Most of us never have the problems of great public acclaim and huge amounts of money, but we constantly need to walk in the Light and be seen for who and what we are—sinners saved by grace who need to watch lest we compromise our integrity and trip and fall. Let us, then, with St. Paul, *"Stand fast therefore in the liberty wherewith Christ has made us free, and be not entangled again with the yoke of bondage"* (Galatians 5:1 KJV).

How Leaders Fall

In Over His Head

At the end, his final defense was, "I was only doing what Jesus would do. I was loving them." What had happened? The minister of the church felt that he had sufficient counselling skills to be of help to women whose marriages were in difficulty. So he made himself available. An attractive woman in his congregation, whose marriage was in trouble, sought counsel from him. He sympathized with her, offered her comforting words, and began to talk of intimate things. Finding her vulnerable, he then moved to touching and hugging. Finally, they entered into full-scale adultery. The relationship continued. This woman was confiding in a friend, who was also in the congregation. She found that her friend was also being "loved" by the pastor. Together they found a third woman whose story was much the same. Feeling embarrassed and used by someone they had trusted, they went to the proper authority. The court proceedings were messy and expensive for the church, and the wounds of the women's marriages were difficult to heal. The minister was removed without counselling. He will somewhere find another pastorate and likely repeat the performance.

The Powerful and the Powerless

We have heard a lot about power in the workplace, in educational circles, in unions, and in the church and how some who have little power accept bullying and abuse in order to keep their jobs. Our friend Titus was not specifically warned by his mentor Paul about getting personally involved in sexual situations, but he did say that leaders chosen for the church must be those who are *"blameless, the husband of one wife"* (Titus 1:6). Church leaders do have power, and the church, which has so much to offer to needy people, can also be the place where much harm can be done. Many have been disappointed when they looked for safety and found betrayal. This is a situation where leaders and followers both must be on guard against inappropriate advances.

Church Fights

The church is, in most cases, a place of safety, but the exceptions make the news. Personal ambition and the desire to have one's own way create great harm and are a rebuke to the name of Christ. Church fights are all too common. Some of the issues over which great fires are started are simply silly. I know of a church that agreed that the choir should have new gowns. After much discussion, the matter of colour came down to a choice between green and maroon. People lined up on either side. The matter of green versus maroon was blown out of all proportion, and a battle ensued. Colour wasn't really the issue; it was about who favoured green and who favoured maroon. More deeply, it was about who liked who. Because they could not come to a peaceful agreement, the congregation was split. Some left, others remained. Later, grudges surfaced when other decisions had to be made. It was a power struggle and there were winners (green won) and losers; but in the end, all were losers.

Doctrines and Other Things That Divide

If differences in doctrine arise in discussion because people have developed rigid beliefs on a particular interpretation of a scripture, then a church may find itself in conflict. Church polity should allow enough space for people to hold reasonable differences in interpreting the scriptures and the doctrines that are birthed in them. But doctrines can be used as an excuse for dividing a congregation. Again it's probably not the doctrine itself but who holds which view that creates divisions. It may be "end times" or differences in methods of baptism. It could be whether children can or can't take communion or whether women can be elders. But lesser matters also can generate much heat. A picture donated in someone's memory may be an atrocious piece of art but "It must be hung in the fellowship room," says the donor. The hour of worship, the location of chancel furnishings, the budget allotments, the choosing of hymn books, the use of guitars or no guitars—all are sufficient to create conflict. A prominent minister came to speak to us in seminary about the ministry. He talked of many things, but what I remember most clearly was his saying, "The devil often gets into the church through the choir loft."

I was invited (or should I say hired?) to mediate a congregational dispute about where a memorial candle stand should be placed in a small village church. It was to be in memory of a child killed in a car accident. I met with the ten people who were to make the decision, along with the child's parents, whose connection to the church was somewhat uncertain. But their desire to memorialize their child by placing the memorial candle stand in a prominent place in the church was very strong. The only item on our agenda was where it should be placed. Some wanted it in the back or at the side; the parents wanted it at the front. We met for two hours in the morning, adjourned for lunch, and then resumed our discussions. Other issues arose; old hurts were revisited. So much "blood on the floor"; so many harsh words spoken. Since everyone involved knew everyone else, who was "in" and who was "out" socially were factors in the discussion. Old wounds were still festering. So many unrelated hostilities emerged. I was amazed that we took so much time over other issues that we were unable to arrive at a satisfactory decision about the candle stand. Too much past history surfaced; too many other antagonisms were exposed. The experience left me exhausted and discouraged. I left with the matter still not settled. I don't know where the memorial was placed in the church, if at all.

Other occasions when I have been asked to mediate disputes all have been difficult. Unspoken issues clog the resolution of broken relationships. When people refuse to be open, hidden agendas cloud a simple issue. Past wounds and continuing resentments fester. St. John wrote, *"If we walk in the light, as he is in the light, we have fellowship with one another, and the blood of Jesus his Son cleanses us from all sin"* (1 John 1:7). If we stay close to Jesus, issues get resolved. Church courts are sometimes justly accused for working in shadows. When a minister is removed from his pulpit, the real issues and the sources of complaint often are hidden from him. The reason probably is that the minister offended a small number of the parishioners. They got together and set out on a lynching. Some of the mentoring of younger ministers I have done has had as its central concern what to do about church problems where the source has reported only, "Oh, you don't need to know all the details."

The Church Bully

The *Toronto Star*, 20 January 2007, carried an article first published in the *Winnipeg Free Press* entitled "Bullying in the Church" by Brenda Suderman. She began her article saying,

"Dominating the microphone at public meetings. Interrupting other people or speaking loudly. Threatening to leave if things don't go their way. Plotting strategies before an event to make sure the popular vote goes their way. This sort of behaviour is most properly described as bullying and it happens all too frequently in Christian churches."

She went on to say that "bullies use their power to intimidate, harass and exclude." Being part of church meetings over many decades, I have seen how decisions are arrived at. It's not necessarily the most sensible choice, or the one that has the support of the majority that wins; but the choice often rests with a stubborn man who has learned how to manipulate the meeting to his ends. Or perhaps it's a strong woman with the spirit of Jezebel who is the manipulator. Sometimes the stubborn one is the minister or the board, insensitive to what's happening in the congregation. It is a rare church that never has problems in its decision making; but bullies must be confronted. Some leaders, too, need to mellow and stop being dictators; others may need to stiffen their spines.

Standing in the Light

Paul was a fighter. Many of his writings to the New Testament churches deal with church brawls. He had no hesitation naming culprits, as well as clarifying issues of doctrine and conduct. He was not averse to taking sides. His most vehement charges were against those who said that Christians must obey Jewish laws. Paul insisted that those of the *"circumcision party...must be silenced"* (Titus 1:11). He warned the Philippian church to *"look out for the dogs, look out for the evil-workers"* (Philippians 3:2).

But there was an occasion when Jesus chose to walk away from deciding an issue. He refused to mediate between two brothers over an inheritance. In Luke 12:13-14 we read, *"One of the multitude said to him, 'Teacher, bid my brother divide the inheritance with me.' But he said to him, 'Man, who made me a judge or divider over you?'"*

FAITHLESS SHEPHERDS AND FAITHLESS SHEEP

He then went on to warn the crowd against covetousness, speaking to the underlying cause of the dispute. Covetousness often is an issue. A good leader will pray to have insight like Jesus into the underlying problems confronting his flock.

13

New Beginnings

Changes

I find that God often wants to rattle the bones of groups, businesses, or institutions that have become sedentary (Ezekiel 37).

A smoothly functioning group can become too comfortable and see change as a threat to their peace. The regulars all know one another and become uneasy when new people appear. "Perhaps they will bring new ideas that would shake the settled routines." I have seen this happen in the church where the old folks said, "We should encourage some younger people to come and join us." But when they came and challenged some of the old guard and their ways, the old folks said, "We liked it better before these new people came." The early church was made up exclusively of Jews, and when Gentiles started becoming Christians and wanted in, the Jewish Christians resisted (Acts 15). We must keep the door ajar and be prepared for some unease when God is doing a new thing. But it must be God's doing, for not everything new is good.

In a different situation, a leader may find God putting His hand on someone in the group, calling him to rise above the pack and take on new responsibilities of leadership. A wise leader will make room for him or release him for greater tasks outside the group. Paul did this with Titus, promoting him from letter carrier to overseer of the Cretan churches. God calls to greatness whom He will. Think of Gideon, who was threshing wheat on his farm when an angel tapped him on the shoulder and conscripted him to lead the Israelite army against the Midianites (Judges 6-7).

In the parable of the talents, Jesus praised the wise investors by saying, *"You have been faithful with a few things; I will put you in charge of many things"* (Matthew 25:23 NIV). Leaders need to be on the lookout for those who have been faithful in performing menial tasks and are ready for greater responsibilities. That same leader may be called to turn over her or his charge to someone God is raising up to move the group on to a new level of maturity and service. When this happens, one needs to have grace to yield without bitterness or unseemly grieving. John the Baptist said of Jesus, *"He must increase, but I must decrease"* (John 3:30). On the other hand, no one should, out of raw ambition, conspire to supplant one in who is in authority. A relevant example is that of Prince Absalom, who wrongly tried to replace his father King David on Israel's throne and civil war broke out (2 Samuel 15 to 18).

Churches in Decline

Not every situation is one of growth or continuity. An urban area with a strong, English-speaking traditional church may experience a surprisingly rapid ethnic change in the population. Many of the church members will move. Perhaps a new pastor may bring to a serene congregation some radically different theological or social viewpoints, which may create an exodus of some who are in violent disagreement. Of course, those who leave take their offerings with them.

There are areas in Canada where the population is diminishing. As a mine runs out of ore, the community around it withers. As sawmills are closed, former workers have to leave the area to find employment. In Newfoundland, when cod fishing died out, fishermen headed to the mainland, many to northern Alberta's oil sands. On the Canadian prairies, where family farms are being bought up by major corporations, the little towns shrink. They lose the local doctor. Then the drug store closes and the implement dealer leaves. The grain elevator is abandoned, and soon the restaurant and school are gone. The pastor of three shrinking prairie churches becomes responsible for five churches as consolidation takes place. The pastor has to deal with a loss of hope among the people as a rural church is closed.

St. Paul wrote, *"Each man has his own gift from God"* (1 Corinthians 7:7 NIV). He also urged each believer to *"Stir up the gift of God which is in you"* (2 Timothy 1:6 NKJV). Perhaps "house churches" are the answer or research into the solutions found by the early pioneers of the area. It takes a special gift to minister to the grieving remnant and help them to find God's answers to the circumstances they may find extremely difficult.

Feed My Sheep

Who would be a leader? My *Random House Dictionary* lists forty-six definitions for *lead*. My first choice among the forty-six is, "Lead: the act of guiding or directing, by going before and showing the way." As He called the twelve disciples, Jesus continues to call men and women into leadership. As He demonstrated in His life and death and resurrection, He has gone before. His Holy Spirit has been poured out to empower His leaders and followers—from Paul to Titus to you, the reader—and show the way.